OLYMPIC ODYSSEY

OLYMPIC ODYSSEY

EMORY CLARK

TaylorButterfield
407 Clay Street
Lapeer, Michigan, 48446

Printed in the United States of America

Design by AURAS Design

ISBN: 978-0-578-15188-5

For my daughter,
LUCY CLARK DOUGHERTY

CONTENTS

FOREWORD

WHEN MY DAUGHTER WAS BORN I STARTED A JOURNAL entitled "Lucy's Log." Part diary, part history, part philosophy, I hoped one day she would read it, and learn something of her early years as well as the life and times of her father. That journal, continued unabated through the years, contained the first draft of this book written sometime in the '80s, when the light, the color, the angst and the passion of that heart-stopping time in a far-away land was fresher in my memory. As the years pass and are now at the half century mark since the Tokyo Olympics, I find I have a story to tell, albeit personal as you shall see.

There is a fascination and mystique about the Games that resonates with nearly everyone, athlete and non-athlete alike. I have confirmed this again and again while reliving my experience at schools, service clubs, athletic banquets, and reunions.

From today's perspective my Olympics was held in simpler, more innocent times. Amateurism was still adhered to (greatly reducing the incentive to cheat) and television had yet to turn the authentic pageantry of many athletes coming together from many nations into an extravaganza in which the athletes seem merely bit players, upstaged by nationalism and medal counts.

But whatever the modern changes, I believe the Games still carry with them an essence, a purity, a concept of perfection that no amount of war, pestilence, commercialism or media hype can snuff out. Most of us yearn for an ideal of human behavior to which we can commit without reservation. The Olympics embody such an ideal even though we know in reality we can never match it. The following pages recount one athlete's attempt, however flawed, to try.

INTRODUCTION

I STARTED ROWING AT THE AGE OF 13 at Groton School, an hour west of Boston, when I was in the eighth grade. Although both my father and brother had rowed, my real motivation may have been that I was lousy at baseball, Groton's other major spring sport.

While awkward at hitting or catching a baseball, I found myself comfortable holding an oar handle, sitting down and going backwards— one faces the stern in a rowing boat. I loved running the half-mile through the woods down to the boat house on the Nashua River every afternoon and messing around in boats—which is pretty much what we did those first few years.

I did not know then where rowing would take me, but it soon blossomed into a passion. I always seemed to be challenged by yet one more finish line.

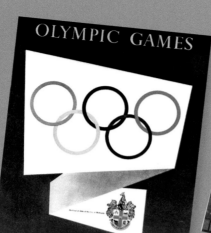

OLYMPIC GAMES

MELBOURNE
22 NOV–8 DEC
1956

XVth
OLYMPIC GAMES
HELSINKI FINLAND
19·VII – 3·VIII·1952

JEUX DE LA XVII OLYMPIADE
25.VIII–11.IX
ROMA

ROMA MCMLX

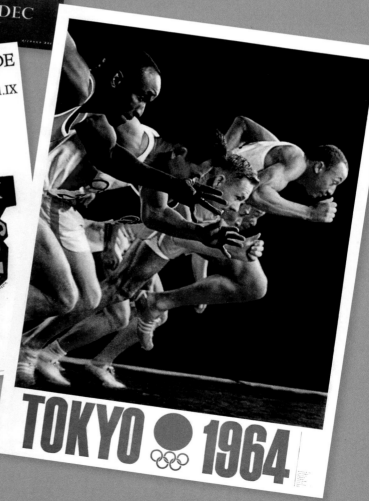

TOKYO 1964

The Spark

DESPAIR. A BROKEN HEART. A LIFE ENDED IN tragedy at a youthful twenty-two. But the flame did not go out completely. A spark remained to light an even fiercer passion that was to rage controlled yet unrelenting all the way to the dark, choppy waters of Japan's Toda rowing course on the other side of the world.

The concept of inspiration born of tragedy, pain, or defeat is not new. History and literature are replete with stories of men and women, nations, and peoples who have found their inspiration in some catastrophic happening, some disaster. In the athletic world, more than one great champion can attribute his success to some deformity, crippling childhood illness, or disabling accident. Men climb mountains because they are there, and those with personal mountains, of whatever nature (the great orator who begins life with a stutter), are in an obscure way luckier than the rest.

I did not recognize it as luck when I indulged in considerable self-pity in the Yale captain's log,[1] perhaps more dramatically than called for by the loss of a boat race. But with hindsight, that debacle on Connecticut's Thames River, the 1960 Harvard-Yale race at New London, can certainly be said to have provided me with a definite edge in the Olympic campaign four years later, a campaign characterized by a certain viciousness in my approach to training, to each stroke pulled, each mile rowed or run, a

1 A journal of each day's rowing kept by Yale crew captains during their senior year.

viciousness spawned no doubt from remembered shame. Losing (seven lengths!) might just have been tolerable, but never again would I permit myself to undergo such an appalling failure of will and courage. Oh, I kept rowing, I kept pulling, pulling hard, but I quit racing, quit trying to convince myself we could bring Harvard back to us. In my mind it was almost as if those two crews out there on that endless four-mile course didn't have much to do with each other, had separate agendas. Any number of early-morning miles, any amount of bone-wearying fatigue

and physical pain was preferable to a repeat of that.

As I reflect now on courage—physical, moral, spiritual—it seems clear that I was dealing then with perhaps the easiest kind, to fight or run, to keep going or quit. Nonetheless, each new crisis of will must be coped with as if one has never been tested. Courage is such a delicate mixture of human traits and emotions that it cannot be bottled or stored for use as needed. You are only as good as your last race, or perhaps, the next one.

But already I digress. If this necessary passion and drive for the Olympic effort sprang from the despair of the 1960 defeat by Harvard, the dream of winning the Olympics had its genesis much earlier.

Photos of Yale team captains in their letter sweaters hang each year in Mory's Temple Bar, established 1849 on York Street in the heart of the Yale Campus.

In July 1956, my brother, Bill, (just graduated from Yale), and I drove from our home in Michigan over to Lake Onondaga at Syracuse to watch Yale beat Cornell by three-quarters of a length in the Olympic trials. Bill, of course, knew everyone in that Yale crew as he had rowed with them for four years, and a couple of them had been ahead of me at Groton School, so by the time I came to Yale as a freshman that fall, I had a bad case of

NEW HAVEN REGISTER, SUNDAY, JUNE 19, 1960

Yale crew captain Emory Clark of Metamora, Mich. congratulates Harvard captain Perry Boyden of Prides Crossing, Mass. after Harvard's victory yesterday. Clark has lost his shirt to his rival in the traditional oarsmen's ritual of betting their shirts on the race.

After winning two of my first three races against Harvard, to lose my senior year was particularly galling. As tradition demands, I had already given my shirt to Kenneth Gregg, my counterpart in the Harvard boat, before shaking Harvard captain Perry Boyden's hand.

hero worship. It was a thrill just to stand on the same dock with them, and occasionally we, the freshmen crew, got a glimpse of them powering by us on the Housatonic River[2] as they tried for their racing edge before making the long trip to Australia that November for the Melbourne Olympics. Then from Lake Wendouree in Ballaarat came the devastating news of the United States' two-length defeat in the first heat, followed by their stunning victory in the final. Gold medalists. Nothing more was needed to confirm in me the conviction that I, too, would row for Yale in the Olympic Games.

When our freshman crew, of which I was captain, was undefeated, I felt just that much more certain of what was already written in the stars, that four years hence when we were all seniors, Yale would repeat

2 Site of the Yale boathouse, an hour west of New Haven.

as the U.S. entry in Rome. My sophomore year, this time in an undefeated varsity boat with four Olympians, did nothing to shake my faith. The Olympics were a reality.

There is not much doubt, however, that even if we had been good enough to go to Rome in 1960, we would have come away empty-handed, as Ratzeburg, the West German eight coached by the great Karl Adam, ushered in a new era in international rowing that year, beating the Canadian crew by open water for the gold. Navy, the U.S. entry and the best of a mediocre crop of college varsities, was fifth in a six-boat final.

Better Navy than Yale, but you could not have consoled me with that bit of logic. I wanted the chance to try, to row my heart out in a losing effort if necessary. But the stars, which I had cruelly misread, did not afford me that chance. As a general rule, it is ten times better to have

My tour on active duty found me in Okinawa in 1962-63. Most of my time was spent in fatigues, or utilities as the Marines called them, almost none in my dress uniforms.

raced and lost than not to have raced at all. Tennyson knew whereof he spoke, even if he did not have athletes in mind.

Since athletic prowess was then traditionally a function of youth, most who lost did not get a second chance. The high school or college senior had to live with the last big game. And if he booted that, well, time dulled the pain, the frustration, the impact of missed opportunity. Five years out, or an entire lifetime, placed it all in different perspective. It was only a game after all.

But I did get a second chance—four years later. And do not think the interim was spent entirely in sackcloth and ashes. At twenty-two, if life ends abruptly through some athletic or romantic calamity, it usually begins again after a good meal and a night's sleep. The 1960 Yale eight did not have much time for mourning as it packed off to England within the week of the loss against Harvard to race at Henley,[3] to lose yet again (Yale man, Jock Whitney, Ambassador to the Court of St. James, had promised the English a crew, albeit a sacrificial offering).

After various tours around Europe, Ireland, and New Zealand, I spent three years as a second lieutenant on active duty with the U.S. Marine Corps. Too many new experiences and challenges for brooding and intro-spection, although I will confess to waking once or twice on the broad bosom of Japan's Mount Fuji or in the steaming jungles of the Philippines with palms sweating from some nightmare race in which my arms turned to rubber or the finish line kept receding. But by and large the memory of that awful twenty minutes on the Thames falling ever further behind Harvard mercifully receded.

---

3   The Henley Royal Regatta on the Thames River outside London.

in August of 1964 and consequently I think that we must sta
start training as soon as I get out of the Marines in
July of 1963. If we had the time we might even qualify
to repre sent the US in the World Championships in 1963
which would be exa ctly the competition that we need.
However I do believe that we should start our sculling
next summer with an occasional row in a pair, just to
get our techniq ue back a nd to get together. You may
not think so, but you will have lost much of the old tu
touch and so will I by then. Will probably even be abl
able to get a n occasional race around New York. Now
we should be running, weight-lifting and rowing lightly
all through the winter, start ing the really serious
work by April. I realize how long this sounds but I know
what this international competition is like and if we fee l
like being in their league at all it is going to take an
extraordinary effort.   B y the way John and I used

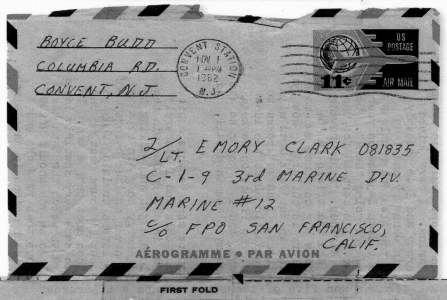

BOYCE BUDD
COLUMBIA RD.
CONVENT, N.J.

CONVENT STATION
NOV 1
1 30 PM
1962
N.J.

US
POSTAGE
11¢
AIR MAIL

2/Lt. EMORY CLARK 081835
C-1-9 3rd MARINE DIV.
MARINE #12
c/o FPO SAN FRANCISCO,
                    CALIF.

AÉROGRAMME • PAR AVION

FIRST FOLD

some of the German interval training methods and I would
like to do that a gain if you agree. I'm afraid that 2 8
strokes a minute won't do. We are going to have to hump
that pair-with coxswain along at about 33 to 35 in the
body of the race if we hope to be in striking distance, b
but that is no problem we will find. Problems: how to get
you stationed in or near New York from next summer on to
the Tr ials; how to get the Marines to pay for part of
the cost of our training program; where to get a really
fine boat a nd the proper oars;   The Rath would be glad
to do some coa ching and there are plenty of places to ro
row, and he will write for you to the Ma rines. Could y ou
get stationed near here? With a will and the kind of
devotion that it will take, you and I could win two gold
medals. Write to me a nd tell me what you think of this .
We must s ta rt now! What do you think, Buddy?   Boyce

CHAPTER 2

Igniting the Spark

IN THE SPRING OF 1962, WHILE I WAS stationed in Okinawa, letters began to arrive postmarked Cambridge, England, describing the Oxford-Cambridge race and various efforts at Henley and in Amsterdam. Enter Boyce Budd, a lifetime friend known affectionately in my family as the Big Budd. Boyce had been a year behind me at Yale and was so big and rough with an oar that after rowing in the varsity as a sophomore he languished for two frustrating years in the junior varsity boat. With a heart equal to his great strength, Boyce was quickly appreciated at Cambridge where he teamed up with Canadian silver medalist John Lecky[4] to help win the '62 Boat Race[5] and then paddle about in a pair (running into log booms and other boats) with John. I suppose Lecky, or someone in England, taught Boyce how to row, but he surely did not learn at Yale. But when he suggested we should train together for the '64 Games in the coxed pair I had no hesitation. His November 1, 1962, letter was bursting with energy and enthusiasm:

> **Dear Em,**
>
> **Well buddy, I know what a bastard I've been not to answer the letter you sent me in Ireland but it ain't like I've been ignoring that**

This letter from Boyce Budd in November, 1962, signaled the birth of our Olympic dream.

4 Rowed in the Canadian eight, which won the silver behind Ratzeburg in the Rome Games, and became a close canoeing and fly fishing friend.

5 Annual four-mile-plus race between Oxford and Cambridge on the Thames from Putney to Mortlake.

letter ever since I received it...We have big things to talk about...I have decided that come Hell or high water I for one am going to be participating in the 1964 Olympic Trials and I hope rowing in Tyoko [sic] or Tokyo...

Em, I could not be more enthusiastic about anything than I am about this and I sincerely hope that you and I can team up in a pair and win the whole lot...Of course this will involve more severe training than you and I have ever done before but I'm sure that we can drive each other on better than most people can...

My suggestion for a training program would involve a prodigious amount of running (up hills especially), a program of lifting weights, fairly light ones where the exercise is repeated many times, much playing of games such as squash or handball to turn two elephantine lard-asses like ourselves into agile oarsmen. Also I think that almost before we touch a pair that we ought to learn to row a single scull...I know from experience that if you can manage a single then you have a much easier time handling a pair...You should get your rowing technique back by finding a single and training in that because we will both be very depressed when we step into a pair and find that we are rowing like two five-year-old kids, and are not gold medalists right off...

We must start training as soon as I get out of the Marines in July of 1963...You may not think so, but you will have lost much of the old touch and so will I by next summer...Now, we should be running, weight-lifting and rowing lightly all through the winter, starting the really serious work by April. I realize how long this sounds but I know what this international competition is like and...it is going to take an extraordinary effort...I'm afraid that 28 strokes a minute won't do. We are going to have to hump that pair-with coxswain along about 33 to 35 in the body of the race if we hope to be in striking distance.

Problems: how to get you stationed in or near New York from next summer on to the Trials; how to get the Marines to pay for part of the cost of our training program; where to get a really fine boat and the proper oars;...Could you get stationed near here? With a will and the kind of devotion that it will take, you and I could win two gold medals. Write to me and tell me what you think of this. We must start now!

Boyce

The spark that had been smoldering for some two years burst into flame. With only ourselves to count on, we knew we could make it—this time we would not entrust our souls to the careless keeping of others, as one must when rowing in an eight.[6] We would control our own fate.

A good many logistical details remained to be worked out. My tour in the Marines was not up until May of '64, and we would have to start training long before that. I had, after all, never pulled a stroke in a pair. We needed a coach and in a general way supposed Jim Rathschmidt, our Yale coach, would be the man. We needed a boat, water to row on, and Boyce would need a job. For most Americans rowing was the most amateur of sports back then, with very little support available for a couple of college has-beens. Certainly there was none in 1963.

At the time I was stationed aboard ship at Subic Bay, an infantry battalion afloat, a pawn on President Kennedy's global chessboard. I was ill-suited for shipboard life and took every opportunity to go ashore. The Officers' Club on the base was almost as bad as the ship, which left only the town of Olongapo. So one night, after a day of small-unit tactics in the jungle, I sought out an Olongapo dance hall (albeit "dancing" at this establishment took on a new meaning when ten pesos and a tip to the management bought you a different kind of dance). There, notebook in hand, I set about to compose a letter to the Commandant of the Marine Corps requesting transfer to the East Coast to train for the Games. I wish

6   In 1964, there were only seven rowing boats in the Olympics, all powered by heavyweight men: Eight-oared crew with coxswain; Four with coxswain; Four without coxswain or straight four; Pair with coxswain; Pair without coxswain or straight pair; Single scull, one man with two sculls; Double scull, two men each with two sculls

I had a copy of it still, as it was, upon the sage advice of my commanding officer, a masterpiece of overstatement. The Marines teach you to blow your own horn, and my final draft showed quite clearly that I was God's gift to American rowing. That letter, the first overt act of my Olympic effort, took a long time to write as I was continuously interrupted by hopeful girls in revealing dresses who felt certain I must be lonely. They were right, of course, but not for them, rather for my friend Boyce and the grip of an oar handle.

The letter, which had to be approved and forwarded through company, battalion, regimental, and division levels, must have taken a long time to reach the commandant's office where, no doubt, it was tossed in some captain's overfilled in-basket for processing. I did not hear anything for almost five months—it was only after I was back stateside at Camp Pendleton, California, and wrote my old battalion commander who had been transferred to U.S. Marine Corps headquarters in Washington that I finally had my answer. Within two weeks of writing that second, personal letter I had my orders—to the Marine Corps Supply Activity on South Broad Street in Philadelphia.

You take what they give you, and the idea of Jim Rathschmidt and training on the Housatonic went by the board. Thank God for that. For while I didn't know it, Philadelphia—and more particularly the Vesper Boat Club[7]—was to become the center of the U.S. rowing effort in 1964. Those orders to the Supply Activity were the first of a series of serendipitous coincidences that were to constitute my Cinderella story with the '64 Vesper eight.

As it was, when I reported to my new outfit on September 3, 1963, I did not know anyone in Philadelphia and had never heard of the Vesper Boat Club. But I knew I needed to row. That day. Boyce still had to find a job, and it would be a month before he could move to the city and we would get an

---

7 Founded in 1865 as the Washington Barge Club and, after a shaky start, reestablished in 1870 as the Vesper Boat Club, the club produced the world's first gold medal eight in the 1900 Olympics, and would become the first men's club to organize a women's rowing team seventy years later in 1970.

apartment together. In the meantime, I lived in the BOQ on the naval base. I called John Carlin, the U.S. representative to FISA, the international rowing body; introduced myself; and told him I needed a single scull[8] in which to start training. He was very kind, suggesting I come down to his club, Fairmount, on the Schuylkill River that weekend and he would see what he could do. Thanking him, I hung up and called Dave Wilmerding, bowman of the '57 Yale varsity, who immediately understood my urgency. He promised to contact Jack Kelly, Vesper's patron "saint," and told me to be at Vesper, also on the Schuylkill, at 5:30 that afternoon.

My new commanding officer had no idea why the commandant had favored him with an infantry lieutenant, but like most Marines, he looked kindly on athletes and told me to take whatever time I needed. He did not need me anyway. So I showed up at Boathouse Row on East River Drive[9] in Philadelphia's Fairmount Park, where, through the good offices of Wilmerding, who had arranged with Kelly for me to use a single, I rowed my first wobbly training mile on the Schuylkill that evening.

That row was the beginning of thirteen months of training, during

USMC Orders for Transfer from California's Camp Pendleton to Philadelphia.

HEADQUARTERS
3rd Battalion, 7th Marines
1st Marine Division (Rein) FMF
Camp Pendleton, California

BATTALION SPECIAL ORDER
NUMBER 68-63

1321/1/RK/rck
1 August 1963

1. The following permanent change of station is effected. TravChar appn 1741105.2752 within CONUS, MPMC-64, OC 21 EAN 74120 Off Tvl, EAN 74150 (Off) Depns Tvl, OC 22 EAN 74152 (Off) trans HHG, OC 12 EAN 74157 (Off) DLA, BCN 43690 within CONUS, BCAN 27. MARCORPER MAN par 9151.7 applies to all Off.

Name	Org	DofD	Report to	By
1stLt CLARY E W II 081825/0302 USMCR	"L"Co	0800 5Aug63	CG MCSA PHILA (MCC 021) w/30 days delrep fordu auth CMC msg 252123Z Jul63 and DSO 223-63 auth 4 das pro 30 das del & 11 das tvl via POC (LvBal 40½ das due) LA: Spring River Farm, Metamora, Michigan. Auth adv tvl	2400 19Sep63

DISTRIBUTION: "C" plus
DPI#
CG MCSA PHILA
RECEIVING ENDORSEMENT

NEIL M. HANSEN
Lieutenant Colonel, U. S. Marine Corps
Commanding

1. Received these orders at _____ Company, 3rdBn, 7thMar, 1stMarDiv(Rein), FMF at _____ on _____ .

8 One man with two sculls.
9 Today called John B. Kelly Drive.

November 13, 1963

Messrs. George & Stanley Pocock
P. O. Box 111 — University Station
Seattle 5, Washington

Dear George & Stan:

Enclosed is a letter from Mr. Glenn Bowlus, whom I understand is a brillant research man, who might possibly have come up with something that might aid our sport. I hope he will contact you and possibly you
could advise him if there is any possibility that his ideas might aid us in
rowing.

At this time I would like to place an order with you for
a new pair-oared shell with cox (cox in the bow), to be built and shipped as
soon as possible to Philadelphia, or at least on the eastern shipment you make
in early spring. This boat will be used for two former Yale oarsmen, who are
actively training for the Olympic Trials. They are, bow, Emory Clark, 6'4",
195 pounds — stroke, Boyce Budd, 6'3", 205 pounds. I personally feel these
boys have great ability and should do a very good job in the Trials. They in-
tend to pay for this boat themselves and have asked me to submit the order
since they are rowing from our Club. I would appreciate your advising me of
the time of delivery and the price.

As you can see from their statistics, they are large boys
and as large a boat as possible should be made for them. In the pair you made
for us, which I believe was one, if not the first, of the pairs of this type,
I felt the seats were placed a few inches too far to the stern, because in
the catch the stern seems to be awfully low in the water. Possibly you have
made slight adjustments since our boat was built. If not, I would like you
to consider moving the seats a couple of inches closer to the bow, or making
the whole size of the boat a little larger. I would like this to be fibre
glass covered to minimize the fragility.

Our boys had a good time in Japan and did fairly well by
coming in a second and a half behind the Germans. We were a deck length behind in the four without and the Amlongs won the pair fairly easily. I hope
we can get an eight together next year that will do as well if not better than
the one we had in the latter part of this past season.

All the best,

J B K J

John B. Kelly, Jr.

At Boyce's and my request, Jack
Kelly ordered a coxed pair for us
("large boys" he describes us)
from George and Stan Pocock in
Seattle—this before Kell had any
thought of our rowing in the Vesper
eight. The boat cost close to $1600.

which I rowed twice a day, six days a week, and lifted weights or ran each night after the workout on the river.

LIFE ON THE SCHUYLKILL

It took me a while to learn to row a single well enough to get a workout. I was up most mornings about 5:30 and on the water a little after 6 a.m. As it was the end of most people's rowing season, I had the river pretty much to myself. Joe Burk, Penn crew coach and great sculler of the late '30s and early '40s,[10] was usually out with some of his recent graduates, who called themselves "The College Boat Club" and hoped to do just what Boyce and I planned to do. Joe would take a look at me two or three mornings a week and kindly offer some tips, but I suspect he thought I was a lost cause in a sculling boat.

About the third day of rowing out of Vesper, I was accosted by a vitriolic little buzzsaw of a man who proceeded to denounce college oarsmen in general—and me in particular—for having no respect for club rowing, claiming we merely wanted to use club equipment and facilities without contributing anything to the club. Up to that point in my rowing life I thought American rowing essentially consisted of college eights and, no doubt, my condescension showed. In any case, Allen Rosenberg, for that is who it was, always felt very strongly about what-ever position he was espousing and was never long on diplomacy. A former coxswain who was Kelly's designated Vesper coach at the time, Allen was living in the boathouse apartment in the attic. I never imagined he would not only become a pivotal figure in our effort but also a close friend. In fact, he left with a Vesper eight for Tokyo that September for a pre-Olympic regatta sponsored by the Japanese, so when Boyce arrived early in October, we had the boathouse, as well as the river, to ourselves.

If not yet famous, Vesper Coach Allen Rosenberg was an outspoken figure in Philadelphia's rowing world.

10 Favored to win the 1940 Olympics canceled by World War II.

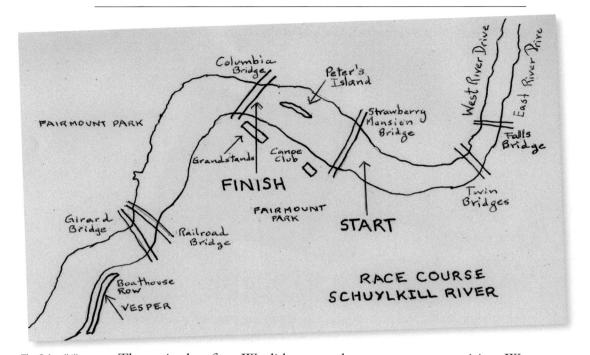

The Schuylkill River rowing course. Over countless miles of practice, punctuated by many hard fought races, every detail of the shorelines became etched in the oarsmen's mental landscape.

That suited us fine. We did not need pressure or competition. We needed to learn to row, to row together and get a start on the training that would allow us to go 2,000 meters[11] full blast. The Schuylkill was ideal for that purpose, always rowable no matter what the wind, and with no powerboat traffic. Occasionally, after a big storm, there would be driftwood, which was dangerous for the fragile shells (made all of wood in those days), especially as we rowed in the dark mornings and evenings in the winter months. It was even more dangerous when I was steering the straight pair (without coxswain[12]), which I did with my foot from the bow seat, looking over my shoulder. Somehow we avoided serious collision.

NOVEMBER 4, 1963—Not a good row, but we've been off the water 4 days. Heavy on the drive and a bad check at both ends. Hard to

---

11 The Olympic distance, approximately a mile and a quarter.

12 It wasn't always easy to find coxswains who were willing to freeze in the dark in those early days.

14

tell how I'm steering in the dark. Should make a move to order a boat this week. Boyce talked to Al about us rowing in the Vesper eight—I wouldn't mind—be a good thing if we turned out to be slow in the small boat. Seems that Al wants to cox too—might be a man for us. Was worried about my arm tonight as it tightened up badly last Wednesday.[13]

We rowed all that fall in the straight pair and moved it reasonably well at times, although I don't remember putting ourselves on the clock. We both realized we were far from Olympic form but were content to keep piling up the miles on the water and working on our technique.

NOVEMBER 13, 1963—Two more hard ones—good row this morning—not nearly as heavy. Was going to come down with Burk's crews but took a start at 2000 meters and it felt so good we went on over the course, then 20 up and 20 paddle to the boathouse[14]—better setup and lighter—called Kelly at work and he said he'd order a pair for us from Pocock[15]—hope he's not booked up. Down over 2000 meters tonight (in daylight) —not all bad—Boyce thought it was down to port a great deal—I don't think so much. Pulled bad to starboard at the start and then to port the rest of the way.[16] Felt better

---

13 I started keeping a training log that fall, much as I had my senior year at Yale.

14 The race course on the Schuylkill is a mile and a half upstream through Fairmount Park from Boathouse Row.

15 George Pocock was virtually the only boat builder in the United States in that era; located in Seattle, he supplied boats for all the colleges.

16 In a rowing boat where the oarsman is sitting down and going backward, starboard is on his left, port on his right. For the coxswain facing forward, starboard is on his right, port left. In most crews, the stroke, the man farthest to the stern setting the pace, is on port but not always. I rowed on the starboard side, while Budd, in front of me, was on port.

In a pair, if both oarsmen are of equal strength and rowing in harmony, the boat will go straight (forgetting about wind, currents, and so on). But if one oarsman is stronger than the other, or his timing is off, a pair (coxswain notwithstanding) can quickly veer off course. Boyce, with his explosive power, used to pull our pair to starboard (against me) in the starts. Later as we settled into our racing stroke, I would pull the boat to port—probably because my timing was off with my oar staying in the water a fraction of a second longer than Boyce's.

physically than last time and my forearm behaved—Burk watched
us a little upstream and said it didn't look like we were getting out
together—good workout if not a smooth row.

Off the water, Boyce was just getting into his job at the Budd
Company, and I, now a first lieutenant, found myself assigned to all sorts
of important tasks, such as designing and acquiring a 150-pound cake
for November's Marine Corps Birthday Ball. We had a reasonably active
social life—dates, football games, and so on—but most workout nights
we ate our evening meal at our Germantown apartment, alternating the
cooking (steak, chicken, pork chops, hamburger, steak, chicken…) and

Boathouse Row, situated on the east bank of the Schuylkill upstream of the Art Gallery, is a National Historic Landmark. It was built largely in the last half of the 1800s and consists of some ten boat clubs. The Vesper boathouse is just left of center.

washing up. We got slightly tight on the one can of beer that we indulged in occasionally, but our biggest gesture toward the senses (other than sex) came Saturday nights when we'd each eat a half-gallon of ice cream.

From the beginning we were determined to leave absolutely no stone unturned on the road to Tokyo, so each bit of junk food that went down did so only after a good deal of internal debate—not that we knew anything about sports nutrition.

Boyce, who had (and has) enormous capacity, used to cheat, but I monitored him closely. Can you imagine thinking that the piece of cherry pie you ate nine months previously would account for that crucial fraction of a second on race day?

It wasn't so much what we ate or didn't eat; rather it was the state of mind, the commitment that went into the effort. We were not, in fact, giving up or sacrificing anything—for that year of our lives there was nothing else we wanted to do. "Commitment" and "sacrifice" are fine words for sportswriters and for lack of better, but we were being completely selfish. Young, unmarried, without responsibility to anyone but ourselves, we could indulge our passion, could concentrate our effort without outside influence in a way few are privileged to do. Asked out to dinner on occasion, we would accept on the condition that we would not get there until 8:30 and must leave by 9:30. To our hostess, it sounded like commitment, but while we were grateful to be fed, we were eager to feel the oar handle again at 5:30 the next morning. We might ultimately be beaten, but nobody was going to have rowed more miles, be stronger, or possess more stamina.

NOVEMBER 21, 1963—We started over the mile course with a couple of prep-school eights and a double—hanging with them till we got washed[17] after a quarter mile. Went back up and came down over the course alone—I had a straight shot but we pulled to port so I had to steer away from the bank under the bridge—we were wobbly and on port but worked hard and laid it on all the way down—we brought the stroke up all right in the last piece till we had to worry about the wall again. Boyce is pretty perceptive in the boat and usually puts his finger right on it when I'm messing up—late out of bow, behind on the sixth stroke, etc.

My log, begun in a desultory fashion sometime in November, indicates that Rosenberg went out with us once or twice that fall and that we were glad for the coaching. As I recall, he did not find much that excited him.

17 Ran into a wake, sometimes from a coach's launch or even from another crew such as an eight.

NOVEMBER 8, 1963—Slow out of bow, low right shoulder, knees up too fast, stopping at the catch end, shifting outside hand on the oar handle, hands too high on the recovery, dipping to the water on the catch—boy you can't beat having a coach—Al Rosenberg went out with us in the launch—first time anyone has looked at us—didn't seem over-enthused—doesn't tend to boost a man's ego.

The only competition we had that fall was a mile race in the straight pair against a couple of Joe Burk's College Boat Club oarsmen. We rowed in an early December snowstorm and managed to win by a length or so. Not an outstanding performance, but we were faster than Burk had expected.

DECEMBER 18, 1963—Friday we didn't get out till after dark cause some Penn guys had the Vampire [all boats had names], a coxed pair. We did all short stuff trying to hit a decent [stroke rate of] 32.[18] It was snowing Saturday when we raced Palms and Robinson, winning by 3 lengths (7 seconds) in 5:53 for the mile—started at 33, then 32 when Joe Burk told us to go down—didn't pull out as fast as I'd hoped. I got a little sloppy in the second half—went up for the last twenty and moved some—it was a real race though—I had that old burned out feeling down in my lungs. Haven't felt that in a long time. There were three races and our time was the fastest by six seconds—tends to make for a better Christmas. I figure we're within reach—we need coaching bad—don't think we've improved much in the last three weeks—hasn't felt really swinging yet—Joe Burk said he hadn't expected us to be as fast as we were—Monday it turned cold but we made it all the way up[19] and came down in

---

18 The stroke rate—or number of strokes per minute. All coaches and most coxswain have stroke watches so they can tell after counting, say, four strokes, what rate a crew is rowing. An experienced crew can hit the desired rate without a stroke watch. Theoretically, the higher the stroke rate, the faster the boat speed—but the sooner a crew will tire.

19 To the Twin Bridges above the starting line, the normal upstream turning point.

intervals—30 up and 20 down—on the last couple it was a grand battle to hang onto the oar—tight wrists. Lifted (sigh). Yesterday we only got upstream to the second barrel and came down in 2 quarter mile stretches—first one was lousy, but the second felt good till we ran into some ice which scared hell out of us. Tired-city. Tonight we rebelled, deciding we were over-trained and went down to the Philadelphia Athletic Club and played 6 games of squash (2-4 Boyce)—sore feet—painsville. But, boy, a look at the old slobs in that place and I'll never call myself a slob again!

The worst weekend of the fall was the one after President Kennedy was assassinated in Dallas. Boyce and I were on our way up to New Haven where Rathschmidt had arranged for us to row against another pair on the Housatonic when we heard that the Yale game had been canceled (as was everything else in the United States that week), so we turned around and went back. Kelly, a friend of the Kennedys, a good Catholic, and a Democrat, closed the boathouse, so we had nothing to do but watch the aftermath on television and go stir crazy. That was a long weekend for a lot of reasons.

NOVEMBER 22, 1963—The President, John Kennedy, was shot (God have mercy on us) and killed about one o'clock. It was hard and is hard to comprehend. My first reaction was how it would affect me personally, right then, there at the Marine Corps Supply Activity, and how it might affect the Yale-Harvard weekend. Straight selfish interest first, and I hadn't even grasped the overwhelming fact yet. I wondered at myself as I thought.

Hard on the heels of that reaction, and while I was still listening to hear that Mr. Kennedy was, in fact, dead, came a sharp unreasoning anger at the men and circumstances that could have caused such a tragedy—and a desire to go down to Texas and kick the shit out of somebody. As the radio played the Star-Spangled Banner after the official announcement of the President's death, I stood at attention in my United States Marine Corps uniform and felt hot and prickly all over.

I was proud to be a part of a proud heritage, and it was only when I learned that the alleged assassin was a Marine (with a dishonorable discharge) that I felt a deep shame for myself and the Corps—a similar shame, I suppose, that the people of Dallas must feel. I thought then that the shooting must have been a result of States' Rights and the Negro issue, and the biting irony of recurring history overwhelmed me.

As I drove home to get ready to go up to Yale, I longed for the eloquence of Abraham Lincoln (thinking of his letter to Mrs. Bixby[20]) as I thought of writing Jacqueline Kennedy with the hope of sharing her grief. I became sweaty thinking of my own insignificance, how history is bigger than us all, and how no matter who or how many I "kicked the shit out of" it would not undo this unbelievable act. I wondered, suddenly, if the Lord had struck down the President for some intolerable sin, and Boyce and I later discussed how most great men usually have their share of sins.

We were fifteen minutes on the road when we heard the Yale-Harvard game had been cancelled, so we turned back—the radio then, and today,[21] is full of reaction from all over the globe and it's easy for me to understand the tears that are being openly shed—curious as I had no particular personal feelings for the President and

20 "Letter to Mrs. Bixby-Executive Mansion, Washington, Nov. 21, 1864-Dear Madam: I have been shown in the files of the War Department a statement of the Adjutant General of Massachusetts that you are the mother of five sons who have died gloriously on the field of battle. I feel how weak and fruitless must be any word of mine which should attempt to beguile you from the grief of a loss so overwhelming. But I cannot refrain from tendering you the consolation that may be found in the thanks of the republic they died to save. I pray that our Heavenly Father may assuage the anguish of your bereavement and leave you only the cherished memory of the loved and lost and the solemn pride that must be yours to have laid so costly a sacrifice upon the altar of freedom. Yours very sincerely and respectfully, Abraham Lincoln."

21 November 23.

was rather opposed to many of his views, but I can feel the same tears within myself. I guess one's feelings can transcend petty fact and grasp the magnitude of a horrible moment in history.

I don't remember taking much more than two weeks off the river because of ice, but from the log it looks like it was more like five or six. The training didn't stop, though. The running and the weight lifting and the squat jumps with a 35-pound disk clutched to our heaving bosoms continued. I didn't mind the running, usually from the boathouse upstream to the finish line[22] and back, three miles, as I could more than hold my own with the others training out of Vesper and was, by the summer, the fastest in the boat. Eighteen minutes, 20 seconds was perhaps my best time, which was not too bad for a big hulk over 200 pounds.

I hated the weight lifting though, hated it and loved it as I knew it was making me stronger than I had ever been, knew that I could attack the water with my oar with three times the ferocity I ever had at Yale. But for all that, Boyce was a third again stronger than me, making it very difficult to stay with him as the poundage went up. By the time we quit the weights—snatches up over the head, cleans up to the chin, and squats with weights on our shoulders—it had become a real mental fight for me. I would think about it all day, psyche myself up, and then attack the barbell. Sometimes the bar fought back and I slammed it down, disgusted. We had no instruction on how to use the weights properly, none of the safety apparatus that goes with lifting today, and it is surprising no one did himself serious damage. Physical pain became synonymous with reaching the goal, and the weights were unrelieved pain, not something you want to do without powerful motivation. We had that.

Over the 1963 Christmas break at Milford, our family property in South Carolina, the highlight of my off-the-water training was a relay race, the so-called Milford Marathon—two miles with lots of hills. I was all

---

22 Where the winner's dock and bleachers were located, and where, four years later, I would ask my wife to marry me.

alone on one team with my brother, Bill, and brother-in-law, Graeme, on the other. Billy took off, out the front drive and around to Tavern Creek on the public road, then passed the baton (a rolled-up *Wall Street Journal*) to Graeme. I was behind by twenty yards or so and Graeme quickly increased the lead, sprinting up the long hill to the back entrance. His uphill burst took its toll, however, and I ran him down by the dog pens, only to discover they had plotted (dastardly deed) yet another switch, for there was Billy, now fresh, urging Graeme to give him back the baton. Graeme waited too long. I got up a head of steam, and Billy, usually a strong finisher, was left standing still. They really never had a chance as I was in pretty good shape after four months of training and no one was going to beat me at anything, not that year anyway. Four years later, they presented me with a plaque on which that old *Wall Street Journal* was appropriately mounted. It now hangs proudly in our house at Spring River Farm, our home in Metamora, Michigan. It was the first trophy of my Olympic campaign. By the time we went back on the water early in February, Boyce and I were ready for the Olympics. The layoff, because of ice, had seemed interminable, and we were more than keen.

In those dreary, cold days of February—both workouts in the dark, the only light coming from street lights along East River Drive—we lived, breathed, and slept under the brooding presence of two guys, Findlay and Ferry, 3,000 miles to the west. We knew if we were going to get to Tokyo in our coxed pair we would have to beat Conn Findlay. A West Coast oarsman, Conn was a legend in American rowing, having won the gold in the '56 Melbourne Olympics in the coxed pair and the bronze in Rome in '60. We knew he was trying again in '64 and, like us, was already training in Seattle. Neither of us knew anything about his partner, Ed Ferry, who later became a good friend, but we figured Findlay could beat anybody (but us) no matter who he had in the bow. So we conjured up an image of him on our kitchen wall and threw mental darts at it all the long winter. On more than one occasion, as we sat eating our meager fare, Budd's huge fist would crash down on the kitchen table with a "Damn it, Em, I know we can beat him." There in the dark night of winter, six months before any competition, we would get so excited we couldn't finish our dinner.

FEBRUARY 4, 1964—Finally hit the water—went out with Al in the old sit-up pair.[23] Boy, did it feel good to get out again. But in the bag after 3 miles. Going to take some doing to get us together. I hope Al can go with us regularly. He talks about punch at the catch end and an even speed on the slide on the recovery. I feel like going to Tokyo tonight—darn! Anyway, we goofed off a fair bit when the ice kept us off the water but kept most of the training we'd picked up last fall—I ran and worked on the chin bar at Milford. We played a little squash and handball back here, but are now in a pretty steady weight program every other day. Figure to lift one day and run the next for the next month or so. Snatches, cleans, leg presses. Just hope we can keep it up steady—Boyce seems to contract occasional back pains, but I need the weights a whole lot more than he does. Al came to dinner tonight.

It was a heady time. We felt the strength and stamina building in us as our confidence in our ability to move a boat increased. Neither the Big Budd nor I were lacking in egos, and in those days the confidence and courage born of hard and harder training were working to make us believe we were unbeatable.

The idea of our being part of an eight, while perhaps in Kelly's mind and floated once or twice by Rosenberg, was not seriously considered. It would grow throughout February and March.

---

23 The new coxed pair we bought from Pocock was designed with the coxswain lying down in the bow as opposed to sitting upright in the stern.

CHAPTER 3

The Boat
Comes Together

TOM AND JOE

WITH THE BREAKUP OF THE ICE, THE PEOPLE who were going to try for Tokyo came out of the woodwork, and the Vesper boathouse saw a lot more use on a regular basis. First, I suppose, were the Amlong brothers, Tom and Joe. They were Army and Air Force lieutenants, respectively, and like me, stationed in Philadelphia so they could row. Like Boyce and me, they were determined to row their pair (without cox) to Tokyo and refused to row in the eight that spring as it was (to use their term) "full of pussies."

Sons of an Army colonel, Tom was born at Fort Knox, Kentucky, and Joe fifteen months later in Haines, Alaska. They were first introduced to rowing in Belgium where their father, the commanding officer of a Graves Registration Unit, was stationed. Shortly after he was transferred to Bremerhaven, Germany, the boys joined the Bremerhaven Rudersport Club where, because they did not want to be separated (the Bremerhaven coach wanted Tom in his eight but not Joe), they persuaded their mother to buy them a double scull. If I had thought about Mrs. Amlong I would have felt sorry for her, but I suppose I was too busy feeling sorry for myself at having to row out of the same boat club with these guys.

When Colonel Amlong transferred stateside to Alexandria, Virginia, the brothers joined the Old Dominion Boat Club on the Potomac, where in the summer of 1954 while rowing in an intermediate eight they were soundly beaten by a Vesper crew stroked by Jack Kelly. Neither Tom and Joe nor Kell (as we called him) could have known the River Gods would conspire to link them together ten years later in an Olympic quest.

That same year, 1954, they enlisted in the Army, joining the Eighty-second Airborne, and then applied for special assignment to train for the '56 Games in a straight pair. They decided they were best suited to the pair because it afforded them the best chance at winning an Olympic berth, or perhaps they realized they couldn't get along with anyone else and no one would be willing to put up with them. Whatever the reason, in the '56 trials they lost convincingly to Jim Fifer and Duvall Hecht, who became Olympic champions in Melbourne later that year.

The brothers then split, with Tom going first to the University of Maryland and then Virginia while Joe was accepted at West Point after having been turned down by the U.S. Naval Academy. As none of these universities had rowing programs, there was a hiatus in their rowing aspi-rations, although each committed to keeping himself in shape. In 1961, after Joe graduated from West Point, they joined Vesper where they lived in the attic and worked in construction for Kelly. Somehow, Joe was in the Air Force by that time while Tom was still in the Army, but they managed to get themselves transferred from Yuma, Arizona, to Philadelphia where they could not only row but get some coaching.

In July 1963 they entered the Henley Royal Regatta on the Thames (flying to London aboard a military air transport system flight), where they borrowed a shell—about which they immediately complained. They created such a fuss about the boat and the races they lost, and with the protest they filed, they were gleefully pilloried in the English press. As a result, when they returned to the United States they were banned from competing for a short time by the National Association of Amateur Oarsmen. Boyce and

I knew none of this when we first bumped into them at Vesper in February of '64. However, it did not take us long to catch up.

Around thirty and twenty-nine years old by that time, the brothers were short for oarsmen, a little over six feet, and each was a solid 200 pounds, enormously powerful with slabs of muscle everywhere—including their brains. Antagonistic and contemptuous of everyone, including each other, they were legendary for their lack of tact. Everyone had a favorite Tom and Joe story.

In sexual matters they were crude in the extreme (one was never in doubt of either's sexual prowess)—Tom in a general, if graphic, sort of way; Joe, who was married, in a more specific manner. While I was never in Joe's house during that year in Philadelphia, for the last fifty years I have carried a picture of his kitchen in my mind. Every day, after they got in the boat, somewhere in the workout, at the top of the island on the way upstream, between the third and fourth 500 meters of the course, under the Strawberry Mansion Bridge, we learned about Joe's sexual activity from the night before. "Took my old lady on the kitchen table last night," or "We did it on the edge of the sink with the water running."

While my sex life was not entirely nonexistent, it was nowhere near as spectacular as Joe's, nor did I share it on a regular basis with all on Boathouse Row. It got so we used to speculate as to what part of the kitchen was honored with Joe's most recent coupling, and, on occasion over the years, when I have had nothing more pressing to occupy my thought, I have wondered about that kitchen (they may have used the bedroom as well, but Joe never mentioned it). How long was that table? How high was that sink? You could write a song. Joe had a pretty low center of gravity, and the thought of the sink would put me in mind of the old South Carolina joke about the five-foot man charged with inappropriate conduct with the six-foot-six girl. In his confession to a skeptical court, the man proudly claimed he used a bucket: "Put the bucket over her head and swung on the handle." While indelicate and distasteful to recall these things now, they were such a part of the climate of our crew and its practices that this reminiscence would be incomplete without them.

Both Tom and Joe were real animals, altogether obnoxious characters who had the facility of having everyone mad at them three-quarters of the time, but whom I, nonetheless, found hard not to like. Sometimes. Tom, in particular, made an effort to be nasty—it being his theory that you would row harder if you were angry and upset. But the most important attribute of the Amlongs was that they were terrific oarsmen and very, very fast in a straight pair. Even so, they could never seem to beat anyone consistently over 2,000 meters. That was because they either consistently psyched themselves out or because Tom, angry for some reason at his brother, would stop rowing, turn around and hit Joe, who quite naturally would falter in his stroke, so by the time they got straightened out, some other, lesser pair would have an insurmountable lead. But they were fast. Nobody in the world that year had more raw speed in a straight pair.

Prior to Boyce's and my advent at Vesper, the Amlongs had had their way about everything, and, I suppose, they found it a little unsettling to find us firmly established in the boathouse when they started training that February. While they quickly set out to establish the pecking order, it soon developed into a standoff—with the test on the river a long way off.

Boyce was so huge that nobody was dumb enough to fool with him, and Tom and I had our little set-to early on. Commenting on the degree of baldness of the various naked figures in the locker room, Tom commanded me to bend down so he could check out my bald spot. Realizing it best to get the intimidation business taken care of early, and with witnesses, I demurred with considerable vehemence, saying something like, "Look you runty little bastard, if you want to see the top of my head you better go get a stepladder." I thought I might have breathed my last, but Tom decided, to the delight of the onlookers who had never quite heard anyone talk that way to him, to let it pass. So the four of us coexisted in the boathouse and were careful not to clash on the river where we had a good deal of respect for each other.

HUGH AND STAN

FEBRUARY 18, 1964—Out in the sit-up pair with Al—went considerably better than the first time. Al doesn't like the way I clear my puddle—don't feather all the way—and says I don't get my power on as fast as Boyce. Rowed bow in a four with Foley and Stan Something-or-Other yesterday and did the same thing. Seemed kind of rushed to me. I'd like to slow down and work on it and Al said we would. Hard to concentrate on details when you are rowing your ass off. The weights seem to be coming a little better—158 lbs. on the snatches now, 180 on the cleans and 360 on the leg presses. Getting a pretty decent workout—my body's in the bag.

Hugh Foley and Stan Cwiklinski, two twenty-year-olds going to LaSalle College, were at the other end of the spectrum from Tom and Joe.

Hugh, born in March of '44 in Seattle, grew up in Montana just south of Glacier National Park where his father was a forester, logger, and farmer—about as far away from rowing, physically and culturally, as one can get. He discovered rowing at Loyola College in Los Angeles out at Marina del Rey where his freshman coach and former Philadelphian, one John McHugh, recommended Vesper for a summer of serious rowing. So, with some like-minded kids, he drove across the country to Vesper and Boathouse Row where Kelly, as he had for so many oarsmen from around the country, found a place for Hugh to stay.

As an outsider, a youngster without pretension (unlike the Amlongs), Hugh kept his head down, worked hard, and wound up in the two seat of the Vesper eight that won the Middle States Regatta on September 1, 1963 (just two days before I showed up on the Schuylkill from Camp Pendleton). The victory qualified Vesper for Tokyo's international sports festival in October, and Hugh went as part of that crew. With probably little notion of what lay ahead but obviously willing to roll the dice, Hugh transferred his credits from Loyola to LaSalle College, which he entered that fall. One of his then classmates and a man from the Fairmont Rowing

Association against whom he had raced that summer was Stan Cwiklinski.

Unlike Hugh, Stan was a born and bred Philadelphian. He played football and fenced at Philadelphia's Central High. Unlike other Philadelphia high schools, however, Central had no rowing team, and a classmate suggested they go over to the Fairmont Rowing Association where Stan could take up sculling. Oars and boats and water suited Stan, and in 1961 he won the heavyweight double scull high school championship. While it is not always easy to go from a rowing boat to a scull, normally scullers can quickly become proficient oarsmen. Stan did. His first year at LaSalle he rowed in the freshman eight, which won the annual Dad Vail Regatta on the Schuylkill—not Harvard, Yale or California, but a very big deal up and down Boathouse Row. How Stan gravitated from Fairmont to Vesper is a bit cloudy, but it seems most likely that his LaSalle classmate Hugh was instrumental in that short trip three or four boathouses upstream. Bill Stowe, who had yet to appear at Vesper from Vietnam, believes Stan first rowed out of Vesper in December of '63 in a four with Hugh, Boyce, and me. My journal indicates that first row was actually February 18, 1964. It matters not. Like Hugh, Stan was big and strong, kept quiet, put up with the often grating idiosyncrasies of the other prima donnas in the boat, and rowed hard.

Neither of them was imposing physically or very experienced, but they trained regularly and hard, and that winter they were about the only other heavyweights at the club. It was not long before we found ourselves going out in a four with them and sometimes even an eight, with Rosenberg either coxing or coaching or both.

FEBRUARY 22, 1964—Last night in an eight—amazing—first time since Henley, 1960. Foley, Knecht, Budd, Clark, Hardegan (he was finishing under his chin), Rose, Donovan and Stan, with Al coxing. Went three miles; I got Dietrich wet every stroke and he complained bitterly. Like the look of Knecht and Foley through the water. Played basketball after, pretty good fun. Out with Al this morning, colder than sin (21°), and kind of windy. Didn't do much going upstream. Trying to work on my catch. I start the rollup, dip for the water, complete with a flip and go in. Need some good water and some low work. Lifted weights afterwards, by the hardest— decided to finesse the leg presses.

AL

We had gotten to know Allen Rosenberg a good bit better over the winter as he was living at the boathouse, and for a considerable time Boyce and I were the only other ones there. Despite lots of complexes, among other things, about being small and Jewish, he was a rowing genius. At the same time he was abrasive, demanding, and arrogant. He frequently had the rest of the rowing world mad at him—either because of jealously at his talent and success, or because he had managed to alienate it by some outrageous demand. That winter Allen had yet to marry and was studying feverishly for the Pennsylvania bar exam. He had been a pharmacist for a while back in the '50s when he had steered several good Vesper eights, usually with Kelly stroking. I don't know how long he had been the Vesper coach at that point, but I think Kelly had taken him on to see if he could harness the Amlongs in some useful way.

He was glad to have a new audience to listen to his grievances and theories. While Boy ce and I didn't always agree with Al, we had great respect and, eventually, fondness for him. Certainly he was the antithesis of Jim Rathschmidt, our Yale coach whom we started out thinking was God.

MARCH 2, 1964—Monday now, we should be out every day. I missed a day on the water in the four last Thursday and I haven't lifted since last Monday because of a pull in my right forearm—think I did it doing one-hand pull-ups—doesn't bother much to row but it balks at weights—convenient, I guess. But, boy, it's bad on the mind—all sorts of fantasies go through my head—a withered arm, etc.—think it's shaping up now though—teach me to screw around. Went out Saturday morning with Rob Zimonyi steering in a fair wind and some chop—rowed nonstop to the top in intervals of 10 strokes paddling, 10 hard, etc. When we turned round Robby said he couldn't tell the difference between the paddling and the hard strokes which was disheartening to say the least. Coming down we were able to please him a little and got a good workout. This afternoon in the straight pair—a horror show—floppy and bad steering. Al says I need more body angle—that I could be 6 inches longer in the water—so be it. Ran three miles while Boyce lifted.

Impressions of that winter and spring are jumbled. We worked hard and harder. Some dark, cold mornings even before starting the workout my whole body seemed tired as I rolled out of bed. We figured it was good for us and we were not happy unless we were exhausted. Each workout brought a moment when it would have been easier just to hold the line, but that was when we drove ourselves to go harder or higher or faster. We looked forward to that point of challenge, eager to meet it, to demolish it, obliterate it. Of all the hundreds of workouts that year, the ones I remember are the ones when I failed to meet that challenge. And they terrified me, so they were few. It wasn't a matter of speed in the water, pounds lifted, or miles run; rather it was a line crossed or not crossed, in the head, a mental thing. I recall one three-mile run when I was way ahead of the rest of the group, but instead of really cranking it up over the last quarter mile, I maintained my pace and let it go at that. I doubt if the difference in my time would have been more than ten seconds, but the difference in effort was light years.

MARCH 9, 1964—Friday in the straight pair—not too bad—went five miles—came down over the last 500 trailing an eight— did a couple of minutes between the bridges—good sweat—then I hurried cause Bobbsie was waiting—saw "Tom Jones" and bed at

0230—bagsville—Saturday up to Elts.[24] Screwed up my arm again somehow over the weekend—worrying hell out of me and I can't lift. Doesn't seem to bother to row, but aches afterwards. Went six with Al this morning—bad 500 at 30—1:51—didn't feel good to me but got up a sweat. Five more in a four tonight with Foley and Stan—not bad—bagged for sure tonight—still some progress—just waiting on the arm now…

BILL KNECHT

Bill Knecht began to show up at the boathouse in March, and while he didn't look like much of a physical specimen, a big barrel of a man, he was certainly a heavyweight. Looks can be deceiving, though, as he was, among other things, the best pure oarsman in the club. Then thirty-four years old with a family of six children, Bill was a sheet metal contractor and had begun rowing competitively in 1948 (when I was just ten). He, like Al, had been in various Vesper eights in the '50s, rowing both port and starboard, and with Jack Kelly had been the U.S. entry in the Rome Olympics in the double scull.[25] Long on experience, he knew what it took to get himself in shape and how to move a boat effectively with an oar. I used to think at times he was goofing off (not rowing as hard as I was) during the workouts, but I kept my counsel figuring he knew what he was doing. Later on I looked to Knecht for leadership, but he never really assumed that role. I think he had seen so much club rowing in sixteen years that the disorganization and squabbling that appalled me just rolled right off him. I'm not sure whom he thought he would row with that year—Kelly had retired—but '64 was clearly to be his last hurrah.

MARCH 12, 1964—Went six miles Tuesday morning in the pair with Al—did a 1:47.5 500 that went great for 300 meters then fizzled. Rowed an eight Tuesday night with me at seven behind Foley—oars tight in

24 Yale rowing friend of Boyce and mine.
25 Two oarsmen, each with two sculls (as opposed to oars).

33

Coach Rosenberg plots racing strategy.

the locks, couldn't feather or pull any water—pissed off. Foley is a good stroke. Went to the doc (Navy hospital) Wednesday about my arm. He said I had some bursitis or a tennis elbow, to keep it cool, nothing to worry about (dumb bastard), and shot it with cortisone. Went in the straight pair Wednesday night and managed to stay with the straight four pretty well—good fun and some good stretches. Tonight out with Al again and I really liked it. Only went three—rowed almost a mile with no feather and had good set-up—my arm better, I hope—ran three with Dave Knight afterwards—feeling good…

BILL STOWE

By no means arranged yet or even recognized, the pieces of the puzzle were assembling. Bill Stowe was the next to the last.

Bill was a blithe spirit. Outspoken in his likes and beliefs, he constantly unsettled his friends with his candor, saying exactly what he felt when he felt it. His charm was that he could do this without hurting people, as his natural kindness and magnanimity of spirit took away whatever sting might otherwise accompany his words. Conservative in philosophy but liberal in emotion, Bill appeared at the boathouse in March, I believe as a direct result of Kelly's string-pulling in Washington.

He was a lieutenant junior grade in the Navy and arrived fresh from Saigon where, with his Cornell hotel administration background, he had been managing the Officers' Club—not an inconsiderable job in that war-torn country which was poised on the threshold of a great influx of American military and had yet to fall to Ho Chi Minh's Viet Cong. But to hear Bill tell it, and his stories were legion, all it involved was orchestrating cocktail parties on the roof of the club to witness each coup as one corrupt regime followed another.

In any case, Bill arrived in Philadelphia to row with the blessing of the U.S. Navy and, despite a large naval installation that might have found a use for him, was not burdened (as was I by the Marine Corps) with any tasks of an official nature. As far as I know, when he was not on the water he was playing golf, working in a brokerage house, or relaxing (which he did very well). Despite his lack of training and considerable bulk (Bill was one of those unfortunates who shows it quickly when he has been indulging himself and always looked as if he needed a brassiere), the stroke seat was his from the beginning. It amazed me how quickly he was able to go all out and how strong he was, particularly since I had a six-month lead on him. Unlike some strokes[26] who are there for their spirit, their ability to pass the rhythm back and keep the stroke up, Bill did all of that and pulled as much or more water than most six men.

MARCH 28, 1964—Last night the eight finally began to move with Bill Stowe stroking. Boyce rode the launch 'cause of a crick in his back. But the damn boat really moved and for the first time I did some work and wasn't rushed. Lying in bed this morning I was getting excited about the eight. We could win everything

---

26 The oarsman at the stern of the boat who sets the pace (number of strokes per minute) and whom everyone else follows.

with that boat if they'd just get organized and not be so damn haphazard. Did a 1:12 quarter. I like Stowe as a stroke (I was seven). The whole thing brought back great memories—an eight can really move—damn that excites me—made the whole week worthwhile—a bad week for sleep. Monday was my birthday party at Carolyn's[27]—Tuesday, three phone calls, the last being Dodie at 11:00 p.m. Thursday Jocelyn came for dinner—we fought and I was mean as usual. Friday, Dodie called again and would have come here from New York, but I said no and finally got to bed all right— but what a mean bastard—have now alienated two good friends. Maybe if I win a gold medal they'll forgive me. My arm has been funny—aching in different spots—but never complaining in the boat. My catch is still a flip—got to learn to slow roll all the way. As I count it up we've only done 190 miles so far this year.

ROBBY

The coxswain situation was desultory throughout the spring. Boyce and I really did not care whom we pulled as long as he could steer and did not weigh more than 110 pounds—the international limit. Johnny Quinn, who was now our coxswain in the pair, steered the eight most of the spring. But Robby Zimonyi was also there, and my log reflects he steered us some. A Hungarian, tall and bandy-legged, Zimonyi had competed in the Olympics for Hungary before defecting to the United States from Melbourne during the '56 Games after Soviet tanks rolled into Budapest. His English was heavily accented, but it didn't much matter what he said; he could steer straight.

Most college oarsmen who rowed in eights took steering for granted until their coxswain went off course or hit a buoy. To have someone you could count on not to lose you 1/100 of a second with his steering—someone to whom the glamour, excitement, and stress of a major regatta meant hardly an increase in pulse—was a great comfort in the Games. If Robby,

27 My older sister who lived with her family out on the Philadelphia Main Line.

unlike Bill Becklean of Yale's '56 gold medal eight, was not the spiritual leader of the crew, if he did not embody the ego of the boat, if he did not possess that intangible quality of spirit that lifts a crew to heights beyond its capability, it did not matter. We didn't need it. We were older, hungry; we had it within ourselves. We needed Robby's experience, his calm, his competence, his ability to steer. At forty-six he had seen it all before.

MARCH 30, 1964—Feel kind of strange tonight—not like it's the big push at all—maybe because it's cold. Those fateful days coming in July and August have receded from my consciousness, while Saturday night when I was with Bobbsie I was ready to kick off the line next to Conn Findlay right then. Maybe it's because both Boyce and I are hurting a little—my forearm hurts as I write, but I can't believe it's bad—played tennis Saturday with Bobbsie and my backhand wasn't much—Boyce has got a back pain and isn't lifting—maybe it's the cold—never be able to tell how much not lifting will hurt us in the final analysis, but we're sort of slipping away from it—would like to start the program again but rowing twice a day it's easy to make excuses for not doing anything more— you have to make your mind up ahead of time and then force it.

Went six miles in an eight Saturday morning—not as good as the night before—different guys, of course. This morning Boyce and I were in different boats—me in a coxed four with Al, Stowe, Stan and Donovan—and Boyce in the Italian straight four. We managed to take them, rowing a 1:36 500 meter piece which was good, and another 1:42 about 4 strokes lower (33)—not so good—hard though—I was bagged.

KELL

For a long time that spring, like the Amlongs, Boyce and I were reluctant to commit to the eight despite considerable pressure from Jack Kelly. The American Olympic eight had always been a college crew (Navy, Yale, California) going back to 1904. We, in our insular arrogance, knew club eights never won at the Olympic trials. Kell, with his years of rowing and Olympic experience, thought he knew better and was determined to put together an eight to beat the colleges.

Kell was the son of a hard-nosed second-generation Irish immigrant who worked as a bricklayer and had won three gold medals in the single and double at the 1920 and '24 Olympics. He later did very well in Philadelphia politics. Kelly grew up with something of a silver spoon in his mouth and a strong parental wind at his back. The oft-told story relates how his father, the original John B. Kelly, had not been allowed to race in England's Henley Royal Regatta because, having worked with his hands, he was not a gentleman. This, so legend goes, is why the old man was determined that his son, our Kell, would not only compete but win at Henley—which Kell obliged him by doing in 1947 at age seventeen and again in 1949. Kell, as we called him (when we didn't call him Money Bags), also competed in four Olympic Games, three times in the single—'48 in London, again in '52 in Helsinki, and '56 in Melbourne—and finally in the double with Bill Knecht at the 1960 Rome Games. His best finish was in Melbourne where he won the bronze.

Kell's most titillating credential was that he was the brother of the beautiful Grace Kelly, movie star of the '50s (before they showed it all and when heroes were still heroes) and, by the time we knew him, Princess Grace of Monaco. While we never saw Grace, she was always there, hovering about in our fantasies, providing some class to balance the Amlongs' crudeness. Kell hated to be introduced as her brother, preferring his own not inconsiderable resume (at least in the rowing world), but he didn't hesitate to use his more famous sister's name if it would give him a leg up, especially with the fair sex.

Of course, we didn't understand or appreciate Kell's role in our effort until years afterwards. At the time I'm sure we felt we were doing him a favor by rowing out of Vesper and were unaware of the myriad logistics it took to put together a top-flight crew. It wasn't until his death that I realized how much affection I had for him. He was a fine man and a jerk at the same time. He spent his life with blue bloods, wealth, and royalty, but he was clearly a bricklayer's son. I remember introducing Kell to a young man at the Head of the Charles[28] years later as I was helping Kell load his single on his car. He was downright rude, giving the young oarsman only the briefest of acknowledgments. As I walked away, I apologized with, "I forgot to tell you, Kelly's an asshole," but in the next breath asserted it really wasn't so, that in the rowing world, he did good things for people. I knew if I called Kell to come speak at the Metamora Lions Club as a favor to me, he would have done it. And given a good speech.

JULY 14 1964

Jack Kelly Jr. getting Olympic badge from his sister, now Princess Grace of Monaco, before the games in 1948.

The New York Times

Our only brush with celebrity came through Kell whose sister, Grace Kelly, had gone from Hollywood stardom to being Princess of Monaco.

But Kell gave more than speeches. He gave his time, his energy, his money, and his name. Shameless and brash at using that name to get what he wanted, he was unselfish in sharing the influence generated by it if it would help an oarsman, a crew, the sport of rowing, or amateur athletics. Thus, he responded in his characteristic way when an unheralded Marine lieutenant turned up in Philadelphia in September of '63 looking for a boat in which to begin training for the Games. From that moment when Kell made it possible for me to row out of Vesper until the Olympic flame was extinguished in Tokyo, he was never very far behind the scenes.

Kell believed in the concept of a fast, mature club eight and lobbied Boyce and me long and hard. He had a point. After all, we were using club boats, club facilities, club coaching, and club water; and, while we knew we were great, or going to be, by that spring we had not won a race in Vesper colors. Another, perhaps more practical, reason for getting in the eight was that in 1964 for the first time the Olympic trials were to be split, with the eight and single chosen in July and the rest of the small boats in August. The hope, obviously, was to produce a stronger overall team, and it provided Boyce and me two shots at the Games instead of

28 Three-mile race on the Charles River in Boston.

one. If we missed in the eight we still had our pair. For all that, we made Kelly promise that even if we won in the eight at the trials we would be allowed to row the coxed pair at the U.S. National Championships against Findlay and Ferry.

After our first row in the Vesper eight, I was dead certain Kelly would never have to keep that promise. At Yale for four years we rowed by fours until everyone's blade work was letter perfect, then all eight at 28 strokes a minute, far below a racing cadence, until the boat was solidly set up (balanced). Finally, well into the season, we might try a 30 or even a 32 if race day was approaching.

At Vesper we rowed a 40 that first day in the eight, and it didn't matter that the boat was continuously down to starboard, we were rushing up for the catch so fast it never had a chance to flop all the way. With my Yale/Rathschmidt background, I thought it was madness but was content to try to keep up (my hands were notoriously slow out of bow) in the evenings so long as we got to row the pair in the mornings—also part of Kelly's deal.

APRIL 2, 1964—No row this morning and what a difference the time off makes! I slept in and didn't go to work till 9 anyway—ate breakfast but was still famished for lunch. Even had a piece of pie—no willpower. It was raining and cold tonight—the kind of day that it would not take much persuasion for you to forget the whole thing. Bare feet are cold on the wet dock, wind drives through your sweat shirts as you lower the boat in the water, and rain goes down your neck. But once you get out and warmed up it's terrific—even if you are rigged low and you get hung up every stroke and Al calls you on your release—I enjoyed it out there tonight—lashing away at the water, cussing Zimonyi and counting strokes—about 350 hard ones tonight in tens and twentys. Dark when we came in and still nasty. Wonderful. I guess it was the rest this morning. Did three sets of squat jumps with 35 pounds clutched to our chests with Dietrich, and five sets of leg presses with Stowe at 400 lbs. Boyce and I seem to be walking wounded: my arm, back and right knee hurt tonight—and I hope Boyce will lay off till Monday—pray that the warm weather will see an end to our aches and pains.

DIETRICH

I don't remember much about who was in the boat throughout that spring. Dietrich Rose, a German from East Berlin who had rowed with Ratzeburg and was another Kelly import, stroked until Stowe arrived. Dietrich, who later coached at Vesper, displacing Rosenberg in typical rowing club politics, brought with him from Germany a good deal of his old coach Karl Adam's training program, which we adopted in part, and considerable international rowing experience, which we valued so highly that we (I should say Kelly) later paid his way to Tokyo as our unofficial team manager.

Dietrich arrived with a lot of rowing and training knowledge, a lively intelligence, an exuberant and energetic nature, and a fine sensitivity, all wrapped up in a heavy layer of Kraut. In keeping with the political correctness practiced at Vesper we called him the Fuhrer. How he, the German who had been just too young for the Hitler youth corps as a child, managed to coexist in the same boathouse with Allen Rosenberg, the prickly Jew, I don't know, but he did, letting Al take the lead while he served as our off-the-water trainer and only came to the fore when Al, for one reason or another, was absent or out of sorts.

It had been Kelly's original intent that Dietrich row in the eight, but despite his many connections in Washington, Kell was unable to get Dietrich his citizenship in time for the Games. Kell even went so far as to suggest that Dietrich marry a black girl from the Philadelphia's Center City, and thus acquire citizenship, but Dietrich declined, telling me years later, "My mother would have killed me."[29]

---

29 I was to row in a four with Dietrich for twenty-five years on the veterans' circuit around the world and treasured his friendship.

The Olympic Trial lineup with Vesper blades. From left: Rosenberg, Zimonyi, Stowe, Knecht, T. Amlong, J. Amlong, Budd, Clark, Foley, Cwiklinski.

THE SPARES

Bill Donovan, a very tough lightweight, made the trip to Japan as a spare, which shows how thin we were. While Bill was a fine oarsman he was not a heavyweight, and when we did need a port spare we turned to Geoff Picard, stroke of the Harvard eight (about whom more, gleefully, later). Chet Riley would show up in the summer and go as our starboard spare.

> **APRIL 4, 1964**—Interesting talk with the Amlongs—find myself in agreement with most of what they say—small boats, competition, etc. They give every indication of being willing to row in the eight—if they feel it's worthwhile. Looking over the field I'd say we have a good nucleus. Foley works; Stan is inexperienced, but wants it; Donovan is a workhorse and rows well; Stowe will be an outstanding stroke, though is not in shape now; Knecht is training by himself but won't slow the boat down. Gus Ignas[30] has started training and will help push us along—an experienced oar. My aches seem to be leaving me—would like to start lifting again tomorrow—with just one workout a day I'm like a caged panther—restless and eager to kill. Boyce hasn't rowed since Wednesday, which means no morning row in our pair, and it's killing him—not worried about him once he comes back—like a freight train and strong as an ox. I was right at 210 lbs. after the row today.

BOAT SPEED

Perhaps because I rowed in the five seat, where, an old English boatman at Henley once told me, "It's all brute strength and ignorance," I never spent much time trying to articulate the mechanics of boat speed. I have since pondered it a bit. Assuming everyone in the boat is in shape and is of a size that gives one the requisite strength, what makes a boat go fast?

Style is one important factor, and there can be as many styles as there are coaches. The best style is that which employs the most efficient use

---

30 Gus, from another era having rowed a lot with Kelly in the '50s, looked like he belonged in a Thomas Eakins painting. I think he worked in a foundry, spent lots of nights in the bar, and more than once showed up at the boathouse in the morning without having been to bed.

of the strength of the oarsman, allowing him to transfer all the power in his legs, back and arms out to the blade that propels the boat forward.

Timing is another important factor. Everyone has to do the same thing at precisely the same time. Each oarsman must take the water at the catch with the oar blade, pull the blade through the water, feather the blade at the end of the stroke, move the oar handle away from the body at the finish as he moves up the slide for the next stroke (the seat rolls up and down on parallel tracks), and square up the blade for the next stroke, all in harmony with the others in the boat. Each part of the stroke must be perfectly synchronized in one continuous fluid motion throughout the crew.

Balance is another critical element. Without the oars an eight oared shell would tip over almost immediately. The oarsman uses the oar not only to propel the boat forward, but to balance it. He may be likened to a tightrope walker with half a balance beam, the man in front of him, his oar on the opposite side, having the other half. As the oar is a lever with its fulcrum at the oarlock, raising or lowering the oar handle even an inch moves the blade out at the end of the 12 foot oar up or down considerably further, possibly throwing the boat off balance. If the boat is unbalanced to starboard (or the right), the four starboard oarsmen will find it difficult to square up their blades and catch the water cleanly, while the port oarsmen have to raise their hands to catch the water without missing the first part of the stroke or "washing out".

Like any other sport which looks easy and effortless when done correctly, there is much more to rowing than meets the eye. A hundred little things can affect the speed of the boat.

If two crews of equal size, strength and heart are rowing the same style and at the same stroke rate in two identical boats, the crew who can make the boat run an inch farther on each stroke will win a 2,000 meter boat race by a very satisfying third of a length. All it takes is one oarsman bobbing his head or slumping at the finish, raising his hands ever so slightly so his blade slaps a wave on the recovery, or coming in a fraction of a second late at the catch, and that inch, and the race, are lost.

The Vesper eight,
ready to race,
leaving the dock.

Spring and Summer '64

SPRING

THAT SPRING MAY HAVE BEEN THE NICEST TIME of the Olympic year. We still had the river pretty much to ourselves in the morning. We were rowing in the dawn now, our workouts lighted by the soft morning sun instead of the street lamps from the Schuylkill Expressway and East River Drive, which had been our lot since November. The spring air was warm, allowing us to shed a layer or two, fingers and toes no longer froze, and it wasn't such an effort of will just to drag ourselves out of bed and down to the boathouse. As the grass in Fairmount Park began to green up and the cherry trees along the river to blossom, so we, with six months of hard training behind us, attacked each workout with renewed exuberance.

APRIL 12, 1964—Friday was a ball buster—six miles with Stowe in the pair in the morning—a so-so 500 in 1:52 but getting better by the time we got back to the boathouse. Then the annual Physical Readiness Test with the Marine Corps at 0900. Was hurting in the three mile run—came in in a dead heat with Major Everett—glad he didn't go any faster. Then 400 hard strokes that night in the Italian eight. Hard to row that seven seat as Gus Ignas pointed out—was washing out some—down on port, but otherwise pretty good. Saturday morning with Boyce at a paddle—first time in a week, but it sure felt good—he's still hurting a little, but we should be going strong in another week—here's hoping—working on boat control so that when we get ready we'll fly!

We already thought we were fast, but the important races were still far enough in the future so that the thought of them lent pique and challenge to the workouts, not anxiety. The moment of truth, the ultimate test, was not imminent, so we could relax and concentrate on getting faster, stronger, and acquiring more stamina.

APRIL 24, 1964—A lot of miles—can't remember much. Boyce started in again this Monday—we've rowed every morning—held the Penn A.C. eight over the last 500 one time—river real high—2:04 and 2:09 upstream for 500, and 1:39, 1:40, 1:41 down. This morning and yesterday we rowed Dietrich and Stowe in the straight pair; did okay at first but today they did better[31]—think we're doing all right though—feels good and light, like it's moving—got to watch my timing—boy, I'm ready.

After our evening outings in the eight, the coxed pair seemed heavy. Everything—pull through, recovery, speed in the water—was quicker and lighter in the eight, so that we were no longer satisfied with the heavy feeling in the pair and worked hard to dispel it. In turn, the small boat helped us in the eight, both because a pair requires a higher degree of rowing finesse—oarsmanship—and because it made the eight seem easy, the oar moving through the water more quickly with the increased speed of the boat. Rowing at 38 and 40 strokes per minute as we were doing all the time in the eight soon dispelled that "easy" impression, but there is

31 The straight pair is a lot lighter boat than the coxed pair, so it felt good to hold them.

no doubt the two boats complemented each other nicely.

MAY 3, 1964—This log closed 'till the Muse catches up with me. I'm too impatient to write anymore now.

The first race I remember was the American Henley on the Schuylkill early in June. That regatta was a critical milestone for Vesper, not so much for what we did (normally sure-handed, I caught a crab and we lost by a length to Joe Burk's College Boat Club eight), but rather because Tom and Joe also lost in their straight pair. They had scornfully, steadfastly refused to row the eight all spring, applying their favorite epithet, "pussies," to those of us who did. But when Tony Johnson and Jim Edmonds, who later became our Olympic pair, beat them that Saturday, the Amlongs were in the eight the following Monday.

They came on their own terms, of course. With loud demands and advice (always given, never taken) for all, they insisted on rowing in the five and six seats and Rosenberg acquiesced, even though it meant moving Boyce and me back to three and four. We didn't care; we knew we needed them, arrogance and all. From the day they got in the boat we began to improve rapidly, moving one to two lengths faster each week. The difference was as much due to their contribution, which was enormous, as to the departure of the men they replaced. With Bill Stowe now firmly established in the stroke seat and Knecht at seven, Tom, Joe, Boyce, and me in the engine room, there was now no weak link. Stan and Hugh, the bow pair, had yet to mature, but they had the basics, were tough, rowed hard, and didn't talk.

THE CRAB

I must take a moment to mention the unmentionable, the agony an oarsman's nightmares are made of, the catastrophe which strikes without warning, leaving shame, tragedy, ruined dreams, and lost races in its wake, the split-second occurrence that can turn a year or a lifetime of training

49

into ashes. I speak, in short, of the crab. Simple enough in concept, a crab occurs when an oarsman fails to square up his blade—that is, have the blade perpendicular to the water before putting it in and pulling. If he does not roll up the blade quite enough as he comes forward on the slide to take the water on his next stroke—if, as a result, the blade slices into the water on an angle—the power being exerted by the oarsmen and the surge of the boat cause the blade to dig a deep diagonal in the water, sending the other end of the oar, the handle, up into the chest or stomach with great force. The result varies depending on the severity of the crab, but none are conducive to speed in the water. At the worst, as a few unfortunates learn each year, the oarsman is catapulted into the water from the force of the oar handle striking his chest. More often, the oar knocks a man over backward on his seat and drags parallel to the boat with the blade under the rigger of the man in front of him. To recover his oar, the unfortunate oarsman must have everyone lean to the opposite side while he wrestles the handle back past his body so he can once again sit up.

Needless to say, while this maneuver is occurring the other crews in the race have breathed one collective "there but for the grace of God…" sigh and have gone on to consolidate their gain. Lesser crabs, ones in which the oarsman recovers without losing his oar, have less devastating effects on the speed of the boat, but even the most minor, junior-grade bobble works to destroy the rhythm or swing of a crew, and often when that is lost, so is the race.

However minimal the physical effect of a crab, its psychological impact can be ruinous. The oarsman guilty of this rowing indiscretion—and "guilty" is the correct word here—tends to become desperate in his effort to atone for his sin (rows harder in a jerky sort of way) and at the same time begins to doubt himself. Fear creeps in, and what are normally automatic, instinctive motions become snares to catch him. So terrified is he lest it happen again, he concentrates too hard, exhausts himself in the determination not to screw up again, and becomes generally ineffective.

While self-doubt is grasping firm hold of the oarsman's rowing psyche, the same sort of doubt is born in the minds of his compatriots. Rowing in all but the single scull is a team sport. The others are important. They cannot win without you, but you certainly can cause them to lose. One of the reasons Boyce and I were so determined to row in the pair was that we did not want to have to count on anyone else. Both of us had had bad experiences in eights at Yale. We each knew the other would stand up under pressure. But when an oarsman catches a crab his teammates begin to doubt him, they worry, they can't concentrate on their own rowing, and the cohesiveness that constitutes a crew, as opposed to eight men in a boat, is lost.

In baseball there is the ninth-inning strikeout, the home run pitch, the three-run error as the routine grounder scoots between the legs. In football there is the dropped pass in the end zone, the missed last-second field goal, the accurately thrown interception, the fumble. In basketball, the sure game-winning layup that goes astray or the free throw that fails to drop. In each situation the team member is singled out for ignominy by his own ineptness, lack of concentration, or plain bad luck. A bad play early in the game isn't always fatal; a bad crab usually is.

In team sports generally, winning or losing is a team undertaking. The crab puts its unhappy perpetrator in the individual tragedy category. Not only has he himself lost the race, missed the national championship, the chance to represent his country, the international medal, but he has lost it for his hardworking, deserving teammates as well. They will, of course, forgive him (publicly anyway—except for the Amlongs). "Don't worry about it, it could happen to anyone." They will be good sports about it, try not to make him feel bad. But their sympathy will make it worse. The crab and its consequences are a heavy burden for any oarsman to bear. As pointed out previously, sometimes the River Gods or whatever deity has jurisdiction over rowing heartbreak will allow the culprit to come back and win the next weekend, atone for the unpardonable and reaffirm his position in the psyches of his teammates. But if there is no next weekend, if the race lost was the final, the last race of the senior year, or any other crucial race, that burden must be borne a lifetime.

Time, of course, puts the crab in perspective. It was only a race after all; one is the same person, has the same human qualities after catching a crab as he did before; life goes on, other considerations, jobs, family, global unrest crowd in to dull the memory. But, if only . . . , if only that one split second when the blade sliced downward could be recalled, that one moment of personal history modified. After all, that stroke had no reason to be so disastrously different than the thousands of others taken in a rowing career. If only he could have that one back, life would be different, and the errant mind would not continue to play that scene again in memory's theater, causing the same sharp twinge of regret.

SUMMER

The summer of '64 is a blending of memory, myth, and sharp and faded images. Apocryphal stories told so many times through the lengthening years that fact is long since obscured. What little memory still serves, the summer really started in late spring, on June 6 on the Schuylkill when our boat lost to the College Boat Club—largely due to the crab, caught, sadly, by me.

The advent of the Amlongs brought character to the boat. Before them we had been an eight, training but knowing the final lineup was not fixed, that there would be changes made. With the Amlongs in the boat there was no one left at the boathouse who might have helped us go faster. While we didn't yet know it, by some accident of fate we had most of the talent on the East Coast in the boat, the fastest eight, coxed four, coxed pair, and straight pair, all in that small group of men. In a way, Vesper served as a national team camp that year, albeit unofficial.

The character introduced by the Amlongs, along with their enormous strength and stamina, was that of the wolf pack. Slash and tear, kill the wounded and the crippled. Perhaps it is unfair to say they introduced it, more accurate to say they made us recognize it in ourselves. By their own self-proclaimed superiority, their constant disparagement of the rest of us, Boyce and I came to understand we were no longer rowing for God, Country, and Mother Yale. Our attitude was not, "One for all and all for one. Take me out, coach, if you don't think I'm doing the job." Rather we were as self-absorbed as the Amlongs; we were rowing for ourselves. We needed them to get there, but we didn't have to love them.

When we were rowing at full power, we were a team, a cohesive team, with common desire, beautiful unity, clock-like blade work. Paddling, in the boathouse, traveling, we were a group of fiercely selfish, if dedicated, individuals. With the exception of Hugh and Stan, each of us had been trying for a long time, each had dreamed and been disappointed. For each this might well be his last try, and no weak-willed pussy was going to get in the way of the goal.

If you thought the guy in front of you wasn't pulling, you told him so in succinct language, suggesting you were going to kick his ass instead of hauling it around the river. Tom Amlong, who was the epitome of mean— real mean—carried this attitude one step further. He thought we would go faster if we were mad, angry, and frustrated. Vicious himself, he wanted us all that way, toward each other and the rest of the world, and he did not need much imagination to keep us spitting venom. We were a little like the New York Yankees in the '70s when Billy Martin was managing. They fought with each other, their manager, the press, and the other teams, all the way to winning the World Series. It does not sound like much fun, but given our fierce desire for the common goal, it did not matter, the boat got faster.

Seems like we raced every weekend in June and July before going up to the Olympic Trials at Orchard Beach, the site of the New York World's Fair. Winning by widening margins in Schuylkill Navy and Independence Day regattas, we garnered cups and plaques and watches, which meant little; the competition was mediocre. We quickly trounced the College Boat Club crew from next door. None of the top college eights entered, but nonetheless we got racing experience and confidence and learned that, even though we never rowed a time trial, never put ourselves over the full 2,000 meters in practice, we could go the distance, starting at 48 strokes a minute and keeping it at 38 to 40 throughout the race.

By that time, with the weight training and the running easing off, our workouts had taken on a pattern—either six 500-meter sprints, paddling three minutes in between, or 600 hard strokes in one big pyramid starting with tens, working up to two 60s and then back down. We never stopped rowing once we left the dock, rowing either full power or dead light the entire workout. There were no half- or three-quarter power strokes, so in a race we only knew one way: Pull as hard as we could on every stroke. There would be no pacing ourselves, we would be in shape to go the distance. No one was going to row the last 500 meters on guts. Courage, I realized then, is in large measure a function of training. If one did go the last 500 on guts, how much faster could one do it on proper training? As a practical matter, when a crew is rowing at 40, each oarsman has to really blast the catch and keep the blade coming if he is going to beat the speed of the boat.

With no time trials (which took a good deal of faith for one who cut his teeth on the Housatonic), we got some notion of our speed by clocking the 500s. Doing six 500s, the idea, of course, was to have the first one fast and the last as fast as the first. With only three minutes paddling between each run, that didn't happen right away. Correcting for wind and water, Rosenberg could tell us within two-tenths of a second what we had done before looking at his watch, and it was not long before each of us could do the same thing. I don't remember the times, but it seems like 1:21 was on the fast end of the spread and 1:24 was dead slow. I do know that after our morning workout in the pair, six 500s at night had us just about crawling up the dock.

The last change in the boat was made shortly after we got up to the Olympic Trials at Orchard Beach—immediately following the first workout, in fact. Johnny Quinn had been steering us all spring, but for some reason not apparent to me he fell afoul of Rosenberg in June and early July, and Al rode him unmercifully from the launch, criticizing his steering and generally undermining his confidence in himself and ours in him. By the time we got to the trials he was a basket case. The lanes on the Orchard Beach course were marked by buoys every ten yards, and for some inexplicable reason from the center of each of the buoys was a little eighteen-inch flagpole with a flag. As these were reasonably stiff, it meant disaster if one were tipped by an errant blade—that is, if the coxswain didn't keep his boat in the center of the lane. Well, Quinny managed to hit two of these flags in our first twilight workout on the race course, and after the second such mishap the Amlongs made a rare joint command decision, yelling, "Out, out, out," in a rising crescendo. It wasn't fair, but we wanted to win and we all felt the same way. So the law of the wolf pack prevailed and Quinny was out, his chance to be an Olympian blasted, his trip to Tokyo a broken dream. In our single-minded drive to our goal no time was spent on the tender sensibilities of any one of us. Rarely has a vote of no confidence been so decisive or the incumbent deported so quickly.

While I think Rosenberg would gladly have accepted a draft for the vacancy—certainly he was of a size and had an abundance of experience steering in international competition—we did not want him to steer us to Tokyo. We wanted him to coach us there. So forty-six-year old Robby Zimonyi was quickly installed at the tiller ropes, and if we couldn't understand him, it didn't matter. He had steered straight in three Olympics for Hungary, and we could tell by his tone whatever he wanted us to know.

1964 U.S. OLYMPIC TEAM TRIALS

TOKYO

Regatta of the
Schuylkill Navy
at Philadelphia, 1874.

ROWING

ORCHARD BEACH LAGOON ● BRONX, N.Y.

JULY 8-11, 1964

FIFTY CENTS

CHAPTER 5

The Trials

HARVARD WAS FAVORED, AND PROPERLY SO. THEY WERE undefeated and, to our delight, had been featured in *Sports Illustrated* the week before. (The kiss of death, I believe—let them write about me afterwards.) California was also unbeaten, but because they were West Coast and nobody knew much about them, the press (much more in evidence than they are today) and other knowledgeable folk went with Harvard. Everyone knew the Olympic eight would be a college boat. It always had been. The clubs were traditionally only strong in the small boats, it being just too difficult to get eight dedicated men with jobs and families and mortgages together twice a day to train.

So nobody paid any attention to us, except Jack Sulger, president of the New York Athletic Club, who was in charge of the trials. He tried to bar the Vesper entry on some technicality—this I assume because of a long-standing feud with Jack Kelly and Vesper. While we knew only a little about the problem, when we left for New York we were not sure we would be allowed to row in the regatta. But we left it to Kell to handle for us, knowing him to be a capable veteran of the athletic wars in which rules and fine print can mean more than speed on the water.

Compared to the college crews such as Yale and Princeton, we were a ragtag outfit, practicing in grubby old sweats, with no uniforms to speak of except our Vesper racing shirts. The Amlongs took special pains to strut about the dock looking muscular and mean. Tom chewed tobacco and spit disdainfully into the water as he muttered loudly about the "pretty pussies," referring in this case to the Harvard crew. He worried not at all about getting them riled up; his tactic was to intimidate. I don't know if he was successful, but from our point of view the Harvard guys did take themselves pretty seriously, acted snobbish and as if they had been reading their own press clippings. That particular Harvard boat had done me no ill and could not know of the indignity perpetrated on me four years earlier by its predecessor. No doubt my conception of them was born of my prior experience in Yale blue. But I had no problem hating this Harvard crew, if for no other reason than those crimson shirts stood between me and the goal that I was driving toward so relentlessly.

I had several anxious and agonizing moments prior to the first heat, waking up in the motel with my back tied up in a thousand painful knots. Unwilling to tell anyone I could barely move, I stayed in bed most of that excruciatingly long day with visions of my year's effort going down the drain and wondering when I was going to have to tell Rosenberg. I delayed that fateful communication until afternoon, finally deciding I would make it to the boathouse before doing anything rash. While the trip and changing into rowing gear involved more than a little agony, I thought I should try a stroke before declaring myself a nonstarter. As it turned out, the only thing all day that did not hurt was rowing. My relief on taking those first few strokes at a paddle was profound—and by the end of the workout the back and its aches were only a terrifying memory. They would reappear in another Olympic effort, but not this one.

The first heat was against relatively weak competition, which put us, after a day off for the *repêchage*, into the semifinals. There we met Harvard, and it was a shell-shocked group of proper young gentlemen that found itself two lengths behind at the finish of what was for us a most satisfying and not particularly tough race. Leaving the "Vards" to the shattered remnants of their invincibility, we went back to our motel with the certain knowledge that a berth on the U.S. Olympic team was ours, assuming none of the hundred possible rowing accidents didn't rise up to smite us in the final.

The Vesper eight as they came from under the Girard Avenue Bridge on the Schuylkill, working to perfect its precision blade work.

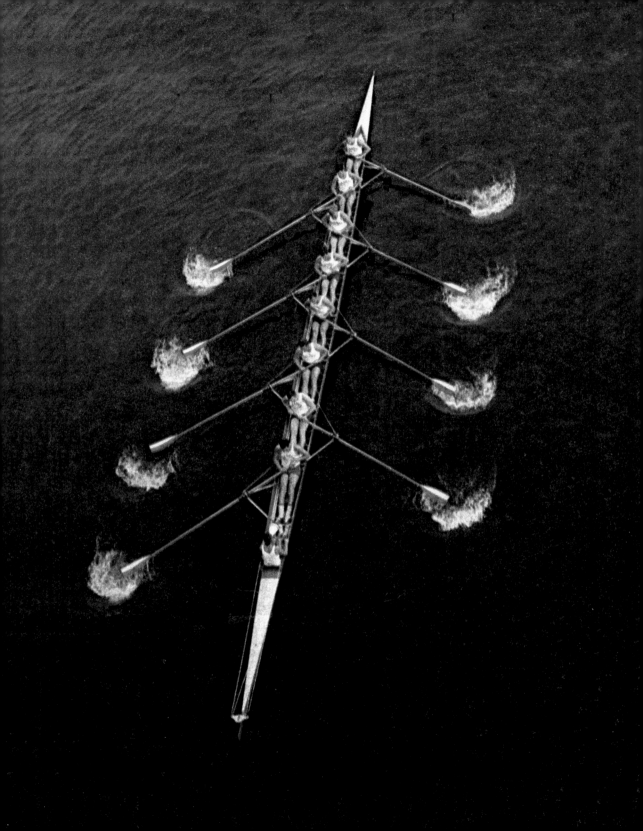

Red Smith 'Twas a Motley But Wondrous Crew

NEW YORK, July 13.

IF THE United States eight-oared crew should win the Olympics final at Toda on the outskirts of Tokyo in October, it would be a charming final chapter in one of the most captivating sports stories of the year.

The United States will be represented by the Vesper Boat Club of Philadelphia, whose crew qualified last Saturday by whopping unbeaten Harvard, unbeaten California and beaten Yale on the Orchard Beach Lagoon up on the northeast corner of the Bronx.

This just doesn't happen. Vesper is a venerable club whose members have been rowing up and down the Spring Garden bridge for donkeys' years. They row for fun and experience and they don't have a burglar's chance against college crews, which are the product of four years' sifting and screening and training by professional coaches.

RED SMITH

Vesper represented the United States in the bush league Olympics of 1904 in St. Louis, and won. Great Britain took the races of 1908 and 1912, but from there on college eights from America had an unbroken monopoly until the wonderful Kiel-Ratzeburg crew of Germany clobbered everybody in 1960.

VESPER doesn't have a professional coach. The skipper is a small Philadelphia pharmacist named Allen Rosenburg, who was Vesper's coxswain for 10 years. The oarsmen are large, gristly characters brought together as a crew about six weeks ago. Three are out of schools that don't have rowing. They are Joe Amlong, West Point '51; his elder brother Tom, from Virginia, and Bill Knecht, 35, from Villanova, a sheet metal contractor with six kids.

Stan Cwiklinski and Hugh Foley are La Salle undergraduates who have never rowed for their college. Bill Stowe stroked Cornell's championship crew of 1962 and since then has done a hitch in Vietnam as a Naval lieutenant.

Emery Clark was captain of the 1960 Yale crew that lost to everybody, and Boyce Budd was on the junior varsity at Yale and the varsity at Cambridge. The coxswain is 45-year-old Robert Zimonyi, a Hungarian refugee.

They ride a 10-year-old Italian shell named for an Irish-American bricklayer, John B. Kelly. Handsome Jack Kelly, who died in 1960, is the patron saint of Schuylkill rowing. He won the single sculls in the 1920 Olympics, the doubles with Paul Costello in 1920 and 1924.

So here came this motley mob from Philadelphia and they weren't even eligible to race in the Olympic trials. They had sent in their entry too late. At a special meeting on the eve of the regatta, the brass relaxed the rules and let them in, seeding them fourth behind California, Harvard and Yale.

Yale never got a call. Harvard led for about half the 2000 meters with Vesper close up and California always third. Then the Philadelphia boat showed its deck in front, and in the last 500 meters drew out to win by a length and a trifle more.

• • •

THEN a slightly sacriligious thing happened. All the Vespers sat up straight and paddled in to the float. This was the next thing to blasphemy Though they take their exercise sitting down, oarsmen are supposed to swoon at the finish.

This is a totem, a fetish, a rite. If you coast in sitting upright like a sailor giving his girl a ride on the lagoon in Central Park, who is going to recognize you as a hero?

No crew ever honored the tradition more dramatically than the Yales who won the Olympic race in 1956. They were pure theater all the way.

They were the first American eight to lose a heat since 1920. They not only lost, they knocked themselves out with a foolish sprint that still left them third, behind Australia and Canada.

In rowing, losers get a second chance, called the repechage. The Yales won this one, beating Italy, Great Britain and France and throwing in a jazzy Ivy League sprint over the last few hundred meters.

This got them itno the semifinals, where all they had to do was finish 1-2. With second place sure, they broke their backs in the last few strokes to bust past Australia and finish first. Three times they had drained themselves, they simply had to come up empty in the finals the next day.

It was beautiful, that last sunny day on Lake Wendouree outside the pretty town of Ballarat in the highlands of Australia. The course was a straight, smooth alley cut through bullrushes near the shore. The Yales took the lead, beat back the Aussies, beat back the Canadians, won, and collapsed. They collapsed singly, they collapsed in pairs, they sprawled in heaps and windrows.

They helped one another down the float to get their gold medals. There they swayed, they staggered, they wobbled, they wilted. It was beautiful. May the Vespers do so well.

Copyright, 1964

YALE (Fourth) **HARVARD (Second)** **CAL (Third)**

VESPER (First)

This Is The Way They Looked As Winning Vesper Crew Neared Finish Line

—(AP Photo)

Vesper 8 Wins Olympic Trials; Cal Takes 3d

Although not so today, rowing made news from coast to coast in the '60s, here sharing the lead headline with the Yankees in the New York Times sports section on Sunday, July 12, 1964.

Section 5	SPORTS	
	AUTOMOBILES—BOATS	
S		© 1964, by The New York Times Company.

The New York Ti

SUNDAY, JULY 12, 1964.

YANKS BEAT SENATORS, 3-2; CARDS (
VESPER'S CREW GAINS OLYMPICS; Q

SPERO ALSO SCORES

Cromwell Is Second in
Sculling—Harvard
Eight Runner-Up

By ALLISON DANZIG
Special to The New York Times

PELHAM MANOR, N. Y.,
July 11—Steered by a 46-year-
old Hungarian refugee and with
Army, Navy and Air Force officers and a former marine pulling four of the sweeps, the Vesper Boat Club eight-oared crew
of Philadelphia qualified today
to represent the United States
in the Olympic Games at Tokyo.

To win the assignment, Coach
Allen Rosenberg's powerful, experienced eight, which averages
26 years, 195 pounds and 6 feet
2½ inches, beat three of the
finest college crews of several
seasons in the final of the O-

6 ERRORS COSTLY

St. Louis Capitalizes
on Poor Defense for
5 Runs in 3d Here

By GORDON S. WHITE Jr.
The Mets once again turned
on the run-making machine in
the wrong halves of innings yesterday, kicking the ball all over
Shea Stadium. They committed
six errors and made other poor
plays that enabled the St. Louis
Cardinals to score an 11-4 victory.

The official total of misplays
marked a season high for New
York. Gaining the most ber

In the interminable twenty-four hours before the final, while our minds pondered each of those possibilities in turn, the outside world discovered us. Reporters called wanting to know who Rosenberg was, what Vesper was. I remember talking for half an hour to some guy from the New York *Herald Tribune* who had obviously put his journalistic money on Harvard and had a lot of ground to make up. In addition, families started to arrive, and girlfriends, most notably Suzy, appeared at Orchard Beach in numbers. (Girlfriends can be one of the possible rowing accidents.) Joe Amlong's voluptuous sister-in-law spent much of the afternoon perched on my bed, which was nice, but not exactly what I needed at that moment. As is always the case, at the time during any athletic event when the athlete most needs to be free of outside distraction, to be able to concentrate, to block all irrelevancies from his mind, he is least able to do so. Vesper was pretty inexperienced at handling the commotion then, but grew better in later years.

Perhaps it was the distraction, our relative inexperience, traipsing around at midnight the night before to find the Amlongs the quart of beer without which neither would go to sleep, or the fact that we had been together as a boat less than six weeks—in any case, we got off to a poor start in the four-boat final with Yale on our starboard, Harvard and California to port. Our race plan was to row in our own boat to the 1,000 where we would take a power ten and then do whatever we had to. With 500 gone, we were a half-length or more down on Harvard, which was making an all-out effort. Being behind did not particularly worry me, but it made me mad, and I was praying Robby would keep his cool and wait until the 1,000 as planned before calling on us. I wanted to row them down and then blow them away when we took our ten. I know Boyce felt the same way—he had only beaten Harvard once in a junior varsity boat in four years at Yale—and the others probably did, too, for their own reasons.

It happened just as I prayed. We were back even or a bit ahead at the 1,000, with all of us waiting eagerly for the word from Robby. Theoretically, an oarsman rows as hard as he can all the time, but somehow during a power ten, called at the right moment, with the coxswain's voice lifting him and counting out the strokes, he pulls harder. Maybe the rate goes up half a stroke, maybe the timing sharpens up, or maybe it's all in the mind, but a big ten is a time-honored rowing tactic, and it worked beautifully for us with Harvard.

I think Robby waited until they had just finished a ten of their own without moving on us, and then we went. And that ten strokes was like the balm of Gilead—it went a long way toward healing a tortured soul—because we moved on them, we shot ahead, gobbling up a seat with each

Harvard understandably featured its loss as opposed to Vesper's victory.

News and Views of HARVARD SPORTS

VOL. VI No. 20   CAMBRIDGE 38, MASS.   July 30, 1964

VESPER CREW BALKS OLYMPIC QUEST
Harvard Whips Yale in Four-Mile; Tops California in Trials

In a corner of the dimly lit boat house, Harvard crew coach Harry Parker choked back his disappointment after the Crimson had lost to the Vesper Boat Club in the finals of the Olympic Trials at Orchard Beach Lagoon.

"We were beaten by a better crew," he said quietly to a small group of newspapermen who had sought him out. "I'm convinced it was our very best effort. We're greatly disappointed that it wasn't good enough to get us to Tokyo, but it just wasn't to be. Vesper is a big, strong crew: perhaps the finest I've ever seen. I'me sure they are best prepared to represent the United States in the Olympic Games."

Crimson adherents who had followed the crew to New York's Orchard Beach Lagoon shared the bitter taste of that moment of defeat. But generally speaking, it faded rather rapidly before the sweet record of accomplishment which belonged to this '64 crew both before the trials, and even during them.

If, for instance, the disconsolate oarsmen took no immediate consolation from leaving California and Yale in their wake during that final row, it is understandable. That old Crimson's did, however, is equally understandable.

Harvard's margin in its "showdown" with the previously undefeated Golden Bears gave the Crimson legitimate claim to having the best intercollegiate crew in the nation this Spring. Add that to a smashing five length victory over Yale in the annual four-mile at New London last month along with the achievements of April and May, and its easy to see why the final feeling about this Crimson boat is one of pride and satisfaction, defeat by Vesper notwithstanding.

Even in defeat, Harvard won the respect of Vesper Coach Al Rosenberg, who couldn't say enough about the Crimson's effort in the final race. "It's a great college crew," Rosenberg said, "and it made a great comeback against us after the way we beat them in the semi-finals."

END OF A DREAM: Vesper Boat Club hits the finish line in Olympic crew trials ahead of Harvard (center), California and Yale.

(Photo by Dick Raphael)

stroke. Just after they had given it their best shot we walked away. Yale was way back on our starboard, and California, unbeaten or not, was never a factor. Harvard was a length behind when we came out of that ten, and I knew then nothing was going to stop us. We were going to win. We would represent the United States in the Olympics in Tokyo.

Harvard must have known it, too, but they stayed game for the last 1,000, which must have been long and hard for them, knowing the bitter truth. We made certain to keep a good length in front, finishing with a little open water.

My memory centers around the big ten at the 1,000; that can still set my pulse racing, my adrenalin pumping. For Boyce it is the fact that we kept on rowing—albeit dead light—after crossing the line, while Harvard collapsed in time-honored fashion. It was nothing more than our normal pattern after finishing our hard strokes, and, indeed, it facilitated breathing, but the contrast was not lost on the 15,000 or so who crowded the bank. The destruction of Harvard was total and complete, and if I derived a kind of obscene pleasure from it, a vindictive catharsis, may God forgive me. At that moment I was convinced that by making the Olympic team in the eight I had forfeited my chance for a gold medal, as Ratzeburg and the Soviets were touted to be unbeatable. And we knew if we could beat Conn Findlay in the coxed pair we could have beaten the world, but now the pair was out. Still, on that sunny July afternoon, stopping Harvard made the supposed sacrifice more than worth it. The Olympics could take care of themselves; for the moment there was victory to savor.

If as a boat we were vicious in competition, we were anything but modest in victory. The paddle to the winners' dock to accept the congratulations of the bigwigs, Vesper supporters, old friends and new, was sweet. Stowe, who often voiced what the rest of us were thinking but did not have the brash (or lack of diplomacy) to say out loud, kept asking where the laurels were and wanting to

know where to get fitted for his Olympic blazer. On the dock there was lots of shoving as we threw Robby in (Quinny now long forgotten), and at least half the boat went for a swim as a score of cameras arrested various moments of our exuberance.

    The scene was repeated at the boathouse after a thoroughly satisfying row up the course in which the crushing victory over Harvard (my

Sports Illustrated from July 24, 1964 Introduces Vesper to the American sports world with a feature spread.

G THAT BOYS

CAN DO

men can do better. That is the fierce belief of the Vesper Boat Club. To prove it, Vesper beat two great college crews for an Olympic berth   by TOM C. BRODY

...since Philadelphia's Vesper Boat ...b first won the eight-oared event ...900 Olympics has the U.S. been ...ted in eight-oared crew by any...t college boys. Last week, in the ...setting of Orchard Beach in The ...wo of the best college crews of —Harvard and California—came ... to settle the question of who ...ow for the U.S. at Tokyo. They ...have stayed at their books. A ...ounch of adults from Vesper— ...gain?—in a dilapidated old shell ...out of a Pogo comic strip left ...arvard and California wallowing ...wake. With a notable lack of in... they had named the winning

shell *John B. Kelly* after Vesper's millionaire-bricklayer patron instead of after his daughter Princess Grace, but this was the only thing the Vespers did wrong all week. "A boatload of men will beat a boatload of boys every time," explained Coach Allen Rosenberg, and Bull Halsey could not have said it any better.

  Rosenberg is a 32-year-old attorney of jockey size who has been coxing club crews for years. Like the Europeans they will face in Tokyo, the time-tested husbands, fathers, war veterans, political refugees and successful businessmen he has combined in the Vesper boat have all grown up with sweeps in their hands and are not particularly awed by the

sight of a burly college boy. "We've seen college rowers before," said one of the club crew last week when an eager reporter pointed to their formidable opposition: unbeaten Harvard, unbeaten University of California, and only twice-beaten Yale.

  Getting the Vesper boat together was slow work; it did not take effective shape until early summer, when Lieutenants Joe (Air Force) and Tom (Army) Amlong rejoined the crew and Bill Stowe, a onetime Cornell stroke, now a lieutenant (j.g.) in the Navy, returned from Vietnam. With the Amlongs and Stowe as his principal pieces, Rosenberg began rearranging his boat like a manic

housewife moving furniture in spring.

  He put Stowe ("the best in the country," he says) in at stroke. Right behind him, at No. 7, he put Bill Knecht, 34, the father of six and a dynamically successful sheet-metal contractor who kept in touch with his Camden, N.J. office during the trials via a shoreside telephone in a white Chrysler convertible.

  Behind Knecht, Rosenberg put the Amlongs, and back of them, at No. 4, he put Boyce Budd, the biggest (207 pounds) and most intense oar in the Vesper boat. A former Yale oarsman, Budd later set a record in pair-oars at Henley while studying at Cambridge. "His style," says Rosenberg, "is classic."

Emory Clark, No. 3, a former Yale and Groton oarsman now working in the trucking business, came to Vesper with Budd. "He caught a bad crab in one race," says Rosenberg, "and he's never made another mistake since."

  In back of Clark sit the two babies of the Vesper crew, Hugo Foley and Stanley Cwiklinski, both under 21. Rosenberg forgives Hugo his youth because "even though his experience isn't as great as the others, he's one of the strongest rowers I've ever seen." Cwiklinski, he says, "has the best bladework in the boat, next to Budd."

  Facing them all at the stern of the boat, steering and calling the continued

...n Zimonyi, 47, calls the cadence for Stroke Bill Stowe, 24, Bill Knecht, 34, Tom

Amlong, 29, Joe Amlong, 27, Boyce Budd, 24, Emory Clark, 26, and the two Vesper babies, Hugo Foley, 20, and Stan Cwiklinski, 20.

The winner's ritual: dunking the coxswain by way of celebration.

subjective view) was still uppermost in my emotions, the fact of being an Olympian had not yet begun to sink in.

Luckily, the general confusion and enthusiasm of a variety of ecstatic well-wishers helped me handle a very serious social situation that there presented itself. Five delectable young ladies, none known to the other, had come, either to share my moment in the sun or console me in defeat. The problem was complicated by my determination to keep my bosom friend, Boyce, in the dark about my amours (he had a similar inclination which I continually foiled that year of our common quest). Except for his sister, Elizabeth, a wonderful girl who, it could be said, might well have come to watch him, her brother, instead of me, I believe I was successful all around. It took some doing. I used my obvious euphoria as an excuse to act demented and leave one girl in one part of the boathouse talking to some friend, while I went off to make arrangements, assisted by harmless white lies, for another. Gradually it sorted itself out and, Rosenberg having given us five days off, I drove into New York City with Suzy where we had dinner with my parents and sister, Carolyn. I spent the night at the St. Regis, going to bed only after the Sunday editions of the *New York Times* and *Herald Tribune* hit the streets so that I could read about our victory—and Harvard's defeat. I note in passing the California oarsmen congratulated us on the dock while giving us their shirts. We never saw the Vards, let alone their shirts.

I mentioned going to bed, but be assured it was not to sleep. I was riding such a high that I did not sleep for four nights. Leaving New York, I went with Suzy to her home in Maine where we ate lobster and walked on the beach and dug clams and played at being in love during the day, while at night I lay (alone) staring into the dark, reliving the race, getting used to the fact of being an Olympian, dreaming about what lay ahead, and, I confess, gloating. As I recall those nights years later, Harvard was as much on my mind as anything, and there was surely something sinful about my feeling. I did not need sleep, did not want sleep.

I did not for a moment want to lose contact with the reality that went with that race, with beating Harvard, with being on the Olympic Team. I re-rowed each race of the Trials a hundred or so times each night and savored the delicious rumor that the Harvard parents and graduates, so confident of victory, had chartered a plane to the Orient and secured accommodations in Tokyo prior to the Trials. I gleefully imagined crusty old Vards at the Harvard Club in Boston harrumphing over the scruffy outfit from Philadelphia that had turned a certainty into a crimson nightmare.

When I did think ahead to an unbeatable Ratzeburg, they seemed too remote to waste much time on. In the glow after the trials, beating Harvard was worth any future sacrifice, and I had a summer as an Olympic hopeful ahead of me. But it was my visceral vindictiveness more than anything that kept me from sleeping—that, and I suppose, the fact that for the first time in ten months I went more than one day without doing two heavy workouts. I am sorry to report it was not Suzy.

From My Brother Bill, an Army Flight Surgeon, About the Trials

Monday, 20 July

Sin San-ni, Korea

Dear Emory,

Many thanks for your vivid letter. Hope you have had time to reassemble your mental apparatus and assess your position, intolerable or not. Even I got excited about your fast crew of assorted nuts. It was good to get the story expanded over what appeared in the Stars and Stripes: it looked like about the third time you threw the cox in. Specialist Kimmerhoc didn't even mention you; he broadcasts the sports news from Seoul. I got kind of dithered about you birds cooling it into the Games. I'm sure the Hamlet in you has pointed out the other side of the cool victor is the second place man who feels foolish wondering what it would have been like if. Hope you get a chance to row in the pairs. Will it be a side race or can you enter in the Olympic trials?

Had a bursting letter from Pa the other day announcing the trip to Tokyo. Carolyn also. I have applied for the 8th Army's quota of first class tickets at the Toda Rowing Course. At present there will be enough doctors around for me to get leave then.

I failed the general on his flight physical today. Am going down to division headquarters at noon to forestall any repercussions if that is possible. My first and last chance to whip it on two stars.

I should have some pictures of Korea soon and by October will have enough stuff to qualify for a press card.

Who is the crew coach?

My best to Boyce and the girl who doesn't wear a bra.

Love, Bill

Korea is beautiful from the air, but otherwise IHTFP.

Take care of your amateur status.

CHAPTER 6

The Nationals

BACK IN PHILADELPHIA, OUR NEXT TARGET WAS THE U.S. National Championships to be held the first weekend in August, again at Orchard Beach. Good to his word, Kelly agreed Boyce and I would row the coxed pair, which meant the Amlongs would go in the straight pair and the bow and stern pairs—Stowe, Knecht, Foley, and Cwiklinski would team up in a coxless four.

During the time between the Trials and the Nationals, not much more than three weeks, we must have rowed the eight some, but the emphasis was on the small boats.

To break up the Olympic eight into small boats as soon as it had been selected was a new and radical procedure, one that must have had the U.S. rowing world more than a little confused, and confirmed its already formed opinion that Rosenberg, in addition to being arrogant, was wacky. The colleges had always had a lock on eight-oared supremacy, and they simply did not have a small-boat capacity. They trained and raced in eights and had too many oarsmen to make effective use of them even if they had had enough small boats—which they did not. The Vesper boat was the first U.S. Olympic eight comprised of a combination of pairs and fours.

The rowing world was still scratching its head over Harvard's demise, however, and, with the exception of a few on the West Coast (Ted Nash, Conn Findlay) and Harvard's Harry Parker on the East Coast, no one had a realistic notion of what it was going to take to beat the European crews.

Looking back, it is clear our small-boat rowing added immeasurably to the speed of the eight, as it increased both our conditioning and our oarsmanship. Karl Adam[32] in Germany had figured this out at least four years earlier with his first great Ratzeburg eight that won at Rome. But there was a big ocean and a lot of psychological water between European and North American rowing.

When we got to the Nationals, Boyce and I had not had one formal race in the coxed pair. We had, however, rowed the Amlongs twice on the Schuylkill. The first time, before the trials I think, we appeared to have the matter well in hand with 500 meters to go when Tom and Joe mounted a furious sprint, making up a length of open water to close to within a foot at the finish line. It was probably a dead heat, but Rosenberg, voting his prejudice, said we won, while Tom and Joe said he was full of shit and quite a few other typical Amlong vulgarities.

In analyzing the race, we realized we had something left and decided we could have pressed harder in the middle thousand. We realized we would have to break their backs early if we were going to escape their truly blazing speed in the last 500—a speed we felt we could not match. They were, I am sure, the fastest in the world that year in the straight pair for 500 meters, and fast enough in the coxed pair.

The next race worked out about as we had hoped, with us building up an insurmountable lead in the middle and coasting home four lengths in front. No one ever squarely beat Tom and Joe, though, and they claimed we had not this time. I forget their excuse—equipment failure, poor steering, something, it didn't matter—we had not really beaten them. We told them they were pussies.

We probably did not learn as much from those two races as we should

---

32 Karl Adam was an innovator in international rowing not only in redesigning the oars from the pencil-shaped blades of the '50s to the cupped tulip-shaped spoons which were in vogue till the '90s, but in having his crews race at a much higher stroke than the conventional 34, thus maintaining boat speed between strokes. This, of course, required a greater level of fitness and stamina in his oarsmen that he attained through interval training—as did Vesper—but was otherwise not much favored in the New World. His eight would win the gold again in '68 in Mexico City.

have. Everyone told us (Findlay's exploits were legendary) that if we were within four lengths of him and Ferry at the 1,500-meter mark we would lose. They would eat us up, walk by us. That was the Findlay trademark; he had done it again and again. We imagined a terrifying sprint like that of the Amlongs and probably should have done our rowing in the middle thousand as we had with them. Later we realized Conn just never slowed down. While other crews were packing it in with a few hundred meters to go, he kept on cruising right through them.

It turns out Conn knew something about us, too, as Penn's Joe Burk was relaying our 500-meter splits to the West Coast where Conn and Ed were training. Conn was quoted as saying that if we were rowing those kinds of times we would beat them, but he did not believe we were rowing those kinds of times. Fair enough.

There were only six coxed pairs entered at the Nationals, so there were no heats, just one final; and it had been agreed by the rowing brass earlier in the week that the winning boat would be sanctioned by the NAAO (National Association of Amateur Oarsmen—rowing's governing body at the time) to go to Amsterdam for the European Championships that weekend. This agreement had been forged through bitter debate with Kelly on our side and Jack Sulgar, venerable head of

Rowing News' round-up of the two 1964 U.S. national champion pairs, with and without coxswain, both from Vesper and both at the heart of the Vesper eight.

ROWING NEWS

VESPER WINS NATIONAL CHAMPIONSHIP TITLE

By Cornelius Peterson

NATIONAL CHAMPIONSHIP PAIR WITH COXSWAIN—VESPER BOAT CLUB
L to R—Stroke—Boyce Budd, Bow—Emory Clark, coxswain—John Quinn.

ROWING NEWS

strong Laconia-Riverside crew which set a wicked pace, rowing 41 for the first 1,000 meters, Harvard moved into the lead by moving up to 40 from a 36 at 1,200 meters with the Schuylkill Navy going to 40 almost at the same time.

The other truly outstanding performance came in the pair with coxswain race as Boyce Budd and Emory Clark from the Vesper Eight beat Stanford Crew Assn. champions in this event for the last four years, in 7:19.7 another gold medal potential time. Stanford was not far behind in 7:21.6 but their form was quite rough. The high quality of these two crews is revealed in the placing of the rest of the field. Third was Detroit Boat Club 18 seconds behind with the rest of the pack thirty seconds afield.

SUNDAY RACES IN HIGH HEAD WIND

The pair without cox, four without and single were rowed under poor conditions making their times difficult to evaluate. A good example was the single row when Don Spero of N.Y.A.C., the Olympic qualifier, beat Seymour Cromwell, New Rochelle R.A. and the recent Diamond Sculls winner at Henley, England, in 7:42.2 with Cromwell at 7:46.7 Three weeks ago under excellent conditions Spero did 7:18.2 to Cromwell's 7:24.7 Spero powered through Cromwell's lead at the 1,000 mark racing a 28 to 30 all the way. The disparity in single times made the pair without race, rowed under the same conditions, look extremely fast. The Amlong brothers, Joe and Tom, racing for Vesper, beat the defending champions from Potomac Boat Club in

7:23.4 to 7:26.1. Reducing this time by the effect of the 20 second wind puts the time in Olympic land 7:00. The national victory was especially tasty for the Amlongs as it was their first in 14 years of competitive rowing even though they have captured numerous other titles including foreign championships and more importantly they row 5 and 6 in the Vesper Olympic boat.

PAIR OARED SHELLS—VESPER BOAT CLUB

The Amlong brothers (Tom—stern and Joe—bow) enjoy the accolade of the crowd for their first National Championship title.

Coxed Pair after crossing the finish line. The winners are still hurting—only Quinny can manage a smile.

the NAAO and the New York Athletic Club, on the other. There was equity on both sides. Conn and Ed would almost certainly be our Olympic coxed pair as Boyce and I were committed to the eight, and it made sense for them to test the competition in an international regatta. On the other hand, if we won, if we were the fastest coxed pair in America, why shouldn't we be rewarded for winning (the American Way), and why shouldn't the United States send its best to the European Championships? The American Way won the pre-race decision, largely, I think, because nobody thought we would win. In eight years no one in the United States had beaten Conn Findlay when it counted.

In addition to being a legend, Conn was six-foot-seven, raw-boned and lean, with arms that hung to his knees. He stroked the pair from the starboard side, and with his coxswain in the bow it seemed like he reached out to the tiller each time he came up to the catch. After nearly a year of dreaming about him, of preparing for him, of imagining the moment, we saw him for the first time in the warm-up before the race.

The Orchard Beach course was flat as a millpond. It took us almost to the 1,000-meter mark to get in our 100 hard-stroke warm-up, but Conn went farther, and, as we paddled back toward the start, an official with a megaphone began yelling at us to get on the line. There were four other boats in the race that had already backed into the starting platforms, but Conn, with the assurance of a two-time Olympian, looked over at us and said casually, "Don't worry, boys; they won't go without us." If I had been intimidated before, and of that there can be no doubt, that innocuous little bit of cool was the *coup de grâce*. I had had a virtually sleepless night and was suffering from incipient cold, headache, and fear. By the time we finally backed into the start, I was without strength, unable to imagine 2,000 meters of supreme effort, and cursing the fate that should render me impotent at the very moment I needed all my powers. At the command, "Row," however, all that anxiety fell away, nine months of training and determination reasserted itself, and the adrenalin that had threatened to overwhelm me was pumping at only maximum level. At the 500 we were a quarter of a length up, cautiously optimistic as we weren't behind—the legend might just be human after all—but frightened we were not farther ahead. I suppose we were rowing a 34 but it seemed Conn was a little above us. When his coxswain, Kent Mitchell, calmly gave them their 500-meter time we knew we were rowing fast.

We had told Quinny, who clutched our tiller ropes, to shut up and steer so we listened to Kent, cool and in control, all the way down. Conn was in lane six on our immediate starboard, thus I was able to keep good track of them, and did, despite rowing's number-one rule—to keep your eyes in the boat.

The middle thousand was just a matter of rowing along a quarter to a third of a length ahead and watching them, our fear mounting as we came up on the final 500, unable to shake them, but not letting them get anything on us. Perhaps we should have tried to really move on them in that middle thousand; perhaps we did and were going as fast as we could. We were so inexperienced we did not know what we could do, how we should feel at each point in the race, but we did know we had to have something left when Conn made his push.

Sunday, August 2, 1964

Harvard Outrows Vesper Fours

By Irving T. Marsh
Of The Herald Tribune Staff

At least half of the Harvard Olympic Trials eight-oared shell is better than half of the Vesper Boat Club eight-oared shell which will be the American representative in the Tokyo games.

After Vesper had scratched its entry in the eight-oared event before the opening of the 90 annual National rowing championships, an event in which it was scheduled to meet the Crimson in a re-match of the final trials, the only confrontation between these two Olympic contenders was the fours with coxswain test.

So yesterday, over the 2,000-meter Orchard Beach Lagon course, in the highlight of the second day's racing, Harvard scored a decisive victory over the Philadelphia shell and did it so convincingly that Vesper was able to finish no better than fourth in the field of six.

Vesper's first title of the afternoon was gained in the pairs with coxswain, a title it was defending although with a different trio than that which won the crown a year ago in Philadelphia. This one had two of the oarsmen from

the Vesper Olympic eight—Boyce Budd at bow and Emery Clark at stroke—with John Quinn, facing forward in the bow, at coxswain.

In beating the Stanford Crew Association, 1962 champions, by a length in 7 19.8, the Vespers turned in the best time ever made in this event in the National championships. Stanford's 7.21.3 at Buffalo in '62 was the previous mark.

Defenders also won the quadruple sculls and the 150-pound fours with coxswain, although once again the boatings were different. The NYAC quartet of Peter Virsis, Frank Sulger, Capt. Wayne Frye and Don Spero at stroke, scored by better than a length over Vesper

The Winged Foot won in 6 24.2. Virsis and Sulger, son of the NYAC coach, were in last year's winning boat.

St. Catharines, of Ontario, had a much more difficult time in defending the 150-pound fours with coxswain, beating the Detroit Boat Club by seven-tenths of a second in 6.58.9

John Welchli, a 35-year-old investment counselor who was the bow man in the Detroit Boat Club's fours without

coxswain that was runner-up to Australia in the 1956 Olympics had a much tougher time winning the 150-pound quarter-mile dash.

Open quarter-mile dash—1, Seymour Cromwell, New Rochelle RC, 1 14.1; 2, Lloyd Martin, Potomac BC, 1.18.6; 3, Jerry Libby, Vesper BC, 1:20.5; 4, John F. Whalen Jr., NYAC, 1:25.1

150-pound quarter-mile dash—1, John Welchli, Detroit BC, 1 18.3; 2, John Sonberg, New Rochelle RC, 1 18.8; 3, George Livingston, Buffalo West Side, 1 18.9; 4, Robert Hardegan, Vesper BC, 1:20.0; 5, Bill Mastalski, 1:21.5; 6, Ed McKenna, NYAC, 1:22.3.

Pairs with coxswain—1, Vesper BC (Boyce Budd, Emery C.crk and coxswain, John Quinn) 7:19.8; 2, Stanford RA, 7:21.6; 3, Detroit BC, 7:39.6; 4, Old Dominion BC, 7:50.6; 5, Laconia RA, 7:52.5; 6, Riverside BC 7:57.6.

Quadruple sculls—1, New York AC (Peter Virsis, Frank Suger, Wayne Frye and stroke, Don Spero), 6:27.3; 2, Vesper BC, 6:27.3; 3, New Rochelle RC, 6:49.1.

150-pound fours with coxswain—1, St. Catharines (John Constantini, John Nickerson, John Dover, Andy Powier, and coxswain Neil Stevens) 6:58.9; 2, Detroit BC, 6:59.6; 3, West Side RC "A," 7:05.8; 4, West Side RC "B," 7·07.6; 5, Ecorse BC, 7·18.8; 6, Penn AC, 7:27.

Associate single sculls—1, Dave Robinson, college BC, 7:21.3; 2, Bill Tytus, Lake Washington RC, 7:27.3; 3, John Bockstoce, Yale, 7·29.2; 4, Jeff Kreger, Wyandotte RC, 7:30.7; 5, Bob Arlett, New York AC, 7:30.9; 6, Lief Goldfredson, Argonaut BC, 7 31

The New York *Herald Tribune*, together with the rest of the press, favored Harvard when it could; here the upset of the day in the coxed pairs was not featured.

The 1,500-meter mark came and went with still only a deck length's lead and our anxiety approaching panic level. When was he going to move, to crank it up, to pull an Amlong on us, to do what everyone told us he would? Without a word or signal, our stroke began to creep up, to 36, to 37, to 38. For once I anticipated Boyce, and we surged forward—they couldn't move on us and maybe we got a foot. With 250 to go we were flying and Kent was talking to them, still in control, but with a note of urgency in his voice, "If you're going to get them you've got to do it now." That "if" did it for us, they were human; Kent had just acknowledged the possibility. Then total panic, our stroke went to 39, maybe 40. I forgot about them finally and worked on trying to finish, to be fiercer, more relentless on the pull-through, to row each stroke harder than the last—to win.

Suddenly it was over, we were paddling, hands trailing in the water, veering off course, unable to talk, but knowing we had beaten the legend. Boyce reached back to grab my ankle and we felt together the fulfillment of a private goal, a personal dream, removed from the public glory of the Olympic team and representing the nation.

National Championship Medal

That was the only national championship I ever won, and I am as proud of that little medal with its red, white, and blue ribbon as I am of the Olympic medal. But it is a private pride, a clean, unsullied pride that means nothing to anyone but me and Boyce and Quinny. The next closest crew was nineteen seconds back—I never saw them. Our time, 7:19.8, was a national record for several years and beat the winning time for the coxed pair in the 1960 Olympics.

Conn and Ed, desperately unhappy, were gracious to us at the boathouse—real sportsmen—and if I mentioned Ed Ferry essentially for the first time, it was only then that he actually entered my consciousness. Conn had so dominated our thoughts, imaginations, fears—indeed, he so dominated the boat—his partner could remain anonymous. But each half of a pair is pretty important, and Boyce and I both came to know and like Ed a great deal in later years.

At that moment, however, our conflict was not yet done as the controversy over which pair would go to the European Championships reared its head again right after the regatta. The plane for Amsterdam was leaving from Idlewild (Kennedy Airport) in just a few hours—and Jack Sulger had the tickets. The bigwigs sat in a circle near the water's edge, as I remember it, and debated the question that they had already decided four days before, while Conn and Ed stood on one side of the group, Boyce (fuming) and I on the other. Clearly, those who had voted to let the winning pair go had never thought we could win, but Kelly, an old hand at the rowing wars, stuck to his guns. Finally, with little more than an hour to flight time and Kelly threatening dire reprisal, Sulger reluctantly surrendered the tickets.

It was a shameful spectacle of athletic bureaucracy, selfish, unfeeling, ruthless, laughable at best—who are these pompous old asses?—tragic at worst. Fortunately in this case the athletes, routinely the innocent victims of this kind of self-righteous "impartiality," were strong enough to withstand the outrage and injustice, to come away, wiser, but still intact. Because of their speed, they were still able to control their competitive fate.

Waiting in the dying summer evening to find out if we would be going to Europe after all, if winning was not enough, if politics and power would carry the day, was a scenario I have seen replayed a dozen times since with a dozen different variations. But those participants were not always as lucky as Conn and Ed. They went home to the West Coast knowing they would represent the United States in the coxed pair in Tokyo, and continued to train. When news of our performance in the Netherlands put them in a deep depression, they just worked harder, and, with hindsight, their loss in the Nationals probably worked to their advantage.

While gracious in defeat, one thing Conn did not do was offer us the use of his boat, a Pocock coxed pair well suited to us, that he had already sent to Amsterdam on the assumption he and Ed would be rowing there. I'm not sure why. I don't think it was so much because we had beaten them. Perhaps he was mad at Kelly for some reason—this despite the fact that he had been on two Olympic Teams (1956, 1960) with him.

An Email from Ed Ferry—Fifty Years Later

From: Ed Ferry
To: Boyce Budd
Sent: Monday, July 01, 2013 2:15 PM
Subject: a visit and an apology

Greetings Boyce,

We had a delightful afternoon, evening and morning with Emory and lovely Christina. It follows an encouragement you made nearly about 40 years ago to visit him in Metamora. We toured the farm in a deluge, told lies, drank beer, relived a crew race or two and agreed what great, full lives we both have had. Your name came up frequently and now I have some bust Budd information lying in wait.

I told Emory and am telling you I apologize for the fact you two did not get to use our boat in Holland in '64. A couple of years ago I again mentioned it to Conn and Mitch and they got defensive, saying Kelly this, Kelly that, he never asked permission, etc. At the time I was the youngest and low man on the totem pole so I didn't say much but over the years it has bothered me. There may have been some sour grapes in there as well. But to deny a fellow countryman their style boat, all of us knowing what kind of work goes into such an effort, is wrong.

Be well. I hope you and I get a visit someday.

Sincerely,
Ed

PRIJS ƒ2,—   F I.S.A.   -   N.R.B.

Europese Roeikampioenschappen 1964

BOSBAAN   AMSTERDAM

Heren 6 9 augustus

Dames 31 juli 2 augustus

CHAPTER 7

The European Championships

OUR FIRST (AND LAST) PROBLEM IN EUROPE WAS that we did not have a boat. That is our official excuse anyway, and it had more than a little validity. In those days before the National Association of Amateur Oarsmen[33] and the National Rowing Foundation sponsored crews every year; before lightweight, youth and women's rowing; before the U.S. National team kept a fleet of boats in Europe—if an American crew wanted to row in the European Championships it had to have the money. If more than one crew wanted to row in the same event, the boat that won at the Nationals made the trip.

The Amlongs won easily at the Nationals over Tony Johnson and Jim Edmonds in the straight pair—the same pair who had beaten them in June causing them to get in our eight, the same pair who would go on to represent the United States in the Olympics. Stowe, Knecht, Foley, and Cwiklinski rowed in a straight four and while they did not win, the boat that beat them did not have, or did not want to spend the money for the trip. So the 1964 Olympic eight went to the Europeans in a four and two pairs, largely, I believe, on money from one of Kelly's friends whose contribution—$48,000, if I recall correctly—did not suffice to supply us

33 Today "USRowing" as rowers are no longer amateur or exclusively male.

U.S. CREWS TAKE EUROPEAN RACES

Gain Consolation Victories —Finals Slated Today

AMSTERDAM, the Netherlands, Aug. 8 (AP)—While the qualifiers for the finals of the European rowing championships rested today for tomorrow's big events, the United States enjoyed unqualified success in races that decided seventh through 12th places.

Boyce Budd and Emery Clark of the Vesper Boat Club of Philadelphia, with John Quinn, as coxswain, earned seventh place in the pairs with coxswain by rowing the 2,000 meters in 7 minutes 49.88 seconds. They beat entries from Bulgaria, Switzerland, Italy, Finland and Greece.

The Vesper four without coxswain also took seventh by winning its consolation race in 6:38.41. Manning the oars were Stan Cwiklinski, Hugh Foley, Bill Knecht and Bill Stowe.

Meanwhile, Don Spero, America's best prospect to win a title, dreamed of a perfect 25th birthday present a victory over the Soviet Union's two-time Olympic champion, Vyacheslav Ivanov—in the finals.

THE NEW YORK TIMES, SUNDAY, AUGUST 9, 1964.

with boats, so we all had to scrounge (borrow) on arriving in Amsterdam.

Boyce and I came up with a coxed pair supplied by Ratzeburg's coach, Karl Adam, who obligingly told us how to rig it. We tried rigging the way he suggested, and, as it did not feel like our boat back home (much lighter on the pull-through), we changed it each workout until we got our old feeling back. Years later, Karl-Heinrich von Groddeck[34] told us that boat was the slowest pair in Germany.

Well, not quite. I think we beat one of five or six crews in our first heat. It was a race that left us angry, ashamed, beaten, and doubting ourselves. It began with a false start, the German pair going on *"prêts"* (the French word "ready" before the starting command, *"partez"*) and then calmly backing down into the starting platform as Boyce and I were still trying to figure out just what the hell all those bells meant. In the next start, our oars gripped fiercely and determined to let no one beat us off the line, we had a disastrous first five and soon found ourselves in fifth place, four lengths behind the Germans. Four lengths! My God! That is what Quinny told us. Further, that we were just behind the Czechs. As I knew there were no Czechs in the race I got so angry I wanted to stop right then to lecture Quinny as to who was rowing in what lane. While I was indulging myself being mad, the Germans and everyone else were increasing their lead, and if we beat anyone in that endless, miserable, heavy row, I don't remember who it was. We finished in deep gloom, put our boat away, and went back to the hotel to lick our wounds and figure out what went wrong.

34 Six man from the Ratzeburg eight who we would race in Tokyo, and three-time Olympian.

On the dock in Amsterdam wondering why, why we were getting beaten every time out.

Our lack of speed was obvious, but the only thing we knew to do, other than not getting psyched at the start and pulling harder, was to change our rigging (if you can't row it, rig it).[35] That was what we did, going part way back to where Karl Adam had told us to be.

We fared somewhat better in the *repêchage*—I learned for the first time what that blessed French word means[36]—but not well enough to make the final, coming in second or third. Thus, we were subjected to what was for us the ultimate ignominy: Being newly crowned U.S. National champions and not even able to make the European finals.

I don't know what we had thought, beyond that if we could beat Findlay we must be fast. But it quickly became apparent that wearing "U.S.A." on one's chest meant nothing to the Europeans who played us like the innocents we undoubtedly were. It was also abundantly apparent that losing with "U.S.A." on one's chest was no fun. By Saturday all we wanted to do was get the *petite finale*—the race for places seven through twelve—over with as quickly as possible and get out of town.

35 Rigging, among other esoteric nuances, meant positioning the riggers on the side of the boat forward or back, adjusting them up or down, in or out, and messing with the oarlock at the apex of the rigger as well. Proper rigging was crucial to the speed of the boat but as it took someone handy with a wrench and the brain of a mechanical engineer, I generally left it to those more gifted—unless it was to complain.

36 Second-chance heat in which the losers from the first heats race each other. Usually the second-place finishers will race third- and fourth-place boats from the other heats to ensure the fastest crews are in the final.

That we were able to win the *petite finale* and a pair of FISA cufflinks lends some validity to our excuse: the boat. By the time we lined up at the start in a drenching thunderstorm, we had put our rigging back the way Karl Adam had first advised and the boat was going faster. I remember little about the race except looking back at Quinny to see him lying in a pool of water with his glasses completely fogged over. A lot of bloody good he was going to do us but, what the hell when you are rowing for seventh place? In fact Quinny steered well and we managed to beat a couple of crews that had beaten us earlier, thus ending on a generally upbeat note and overcoming our initial response to Thomas Keller's[37] cufflinks—which was to throw them in the Bosbaan, Amsterdam's man-made rowing course. We had played it straight, however (unlike the Australians who tend to get roaring drunk the night before if they find themselves in the *petite finale*), and had rowed, finally, a respectable race.

The night after was a different story. I learned then that if you are there to see the sights and have a good time, it is best to lose early in the week. She stopped me on my way through the hotel lobby to ask why I looked so sad. As that would have taken too long to tell, and as I was willing to share my body with a stranger, but not my soul, I smiled and agreed to let her show me the jazz spots in Amsterdam.

Budd, whose Irish love, Rose Marie, had been calling him from Paris at all hours of the night, generally increasing my wrath at him and the world in general, could not believe it when I failed to join him in misery at the training table that evening. In fact, I did not reappear until Sunday morning just in time for the finals.

And that was a near-run thing. When my mood did not improve noticeably, when I found the jazz too loud, when it became apparent my dancing was a disaster, that this American, in short, was not a Hollywood swinger, my pretty Dutch girl, who was working as a clerk in the rowing

---

37 Head of the Fédération Internationale des Sociétés d'Aviron, FISA, who eight years earlier as a Swiss sculler had been picked to row in the '56 Melbourne Olympics but was denied when Switzerland boycotted those Games to protest the Soviet Union's invasion of Hungary.

Good manners prevail in accepting seventh-place cufflinks from Thomas Keller.

hotel, almost threw in the towel. But she had made her bed and apparently did not want to lie in it alone. So as our taxi paused by the hotel and I rather ungallantly asked if I should stay or go, she responded with a shrug, "You might as well stay." Her decision was anything but passionate though I thought I performed credibly enough on a narrow bed in an apartment belonging to others. I recall sneaking in and out. But the following night she chose another American who shall remain nameless and I was left to attend the regatta ball.

The finals, which I watched unhappily from the stands, were memorable for two races. In the straight pair, the Dutch came out of nowhere like a whirling dervish to overtake another crew at the wire, leaving a delirious home crowd gasping. It was the kind of race that brings tears to the eyes no matter what your nationality, as you can't help but be caught up by the fervor of the crowd and the magnificent effort of both winners and losers.

The Amlongs were also in that race, almost four lengths in front of the field at the 1,000-meter mark, then fading to finish fourth, way out of their lane. Tom had been particularly obnoxious all week, telling everyone he could buttonhole—and he was never reticent—that Joe was a "pussy," and more specifically that, "my brother craps out at the 1,000." I suppose Joe started believing it, because sure enough, at the halfway mark with a comfortable lead, their pair took an almost right angle turn to starboard and crossed four lanes. And, sure enough, when they pulled into the dock Tom's first words were, "My brother crapped out at the 1,000." Tom and Joe would have been the fastest pair in the world that year if they could have put it together in their heads.

The eight race between the Germans and the Soviet Union was another I'll never forget. It was awe inspiring from any objective point of view, and knowing I was going to have to race both of those magnificent crews in a few months' time changed that awe into near terror. Both boats rowed 40 all the way, never faltering, with the Soviets leading by a few hundredths of a second at each 500-meter mark. I suppose both crews sprinted (it is hard to know where you go from a 40), and they churned by the stands dead even, neither willing to blink, to give an inch, in what looked to be a dead heat. But the clock gave victory to Ratzeburg by 2/100s of a second, a victory that was to have profound repercussions in Tokyo in the coming October.

There is no doubt the American Olympic eight, which had raced with something less than distinction in Amsterdam, went home a much wiser and more humble crew. The straight four of Stowe, Knecht, Foley, and Cwiklinski won the *petite finale* as did Boyce and I. This, sadly, allowed the Amlongs to crow even louder—they never needed an excuse—as they were the only ones to make the final. Thank God they hadn't won.

In any case, we had gotten our first dose of international competition. We had heard the *"Etes vous prêts"* (Are you ready)? We knew now what it was like to boil off the start with coxswains screaming in the six different languages. We learned how difficult concentration would be in the excitement of gathering with the world's greatest athletes. We knew we had to ignore the incessant talk, the psyching efforts that attend any such gathering. We soaked it all up. None of it would be new or distracting in Tokyo.

Most important, we had that one crucial look at the competition—something to take home and dream about over the coming days and weeks. We did not have to imagine it any more. We had seen it. It was there in the mind's eye. We would not arrive in Tokyo with any self-delusion derived from our speed on home waters. Beating Harvard would not even get us in the finals in Japan. Ratzeburg was not a myth; they were real and really fast. And the Soviets were just as fast. In Amsterdam we finally learned the game—and were forcibly reminded how rotten it feels to lose. Both were to stand us in good stead.

The Tokyo line up (with the Amlongs in their final seats at four and bow) back home at Vesper getting ready to race Ratzeburg.

CHAPTER 8

Late Summer

MOST OF US DREAM OF BEING HEROES BUT settle for having them. But the right kind of hero is in short supply. Americans feel good about their Olympic athletes and are content to make them heroes. The Olympic year is the one time an athlete does not have to be a football or basketball star to gain public interest and recognition. There is a mystique that goes with the word "Olympic," a luster that penetrates the intellect of even the most non-sports-minded person. Being a hero is a function of the perceptions (or misperceptions) of other people—one is measured by their standard, not the interior standard one sets for one's self.

The weeks between returning from Amsterdam and leaving for Tokyo were my time to be a hero. It had to be then, as I planned to go on around the world after Tokyo, and did not, in fact, return to the North American continent for nine months. In retrospect it seems good to be a hero and to bask in the warm approbation of one's fellow man before one does whatever it is that is going to make one heroic. The soldier marching in the postwar victory parade knows, despite all the confetti, cheering, and martial music, that war is an unbelievably inhumane hell and that he is lucky just to have survived. The athlete after the race, no matter how great the victory, just for a brief time or perhaps all time, faces an emptiness, a vacuum, a life without the all-important finish line toward which to strive.

It was fun to share the fact that I was an Olympic athlete with the everyday people I bumped into, to give them the pleasure of meeting me, thus a more personal stake in the Olympic news from faraway Tokyo, and to go away with their sincere good wishes. Normally my natural reticence and, perhaps, false modesty would have served to keep me from revealing my Olympic status—but when I realized how much joy it gave people, I overcame it. As I planned to go on from Japan, I spent considerable time looking for and purchasing large-scale maps of such places as Indonesia, India, Pakistan, and Africa. The man who sold them to me grew positively patriotic when he learned I was on the team and paid the sales tax on my maps from his own till. Not a large gesture, but a genuine one. Upon inquiry at the Philadelphia Art Gallery for some Thomas Eakins rowing prints, the young woman behind the counter became more than a little interested and subsequently traced me through a picture of the crew in the *Philadelphia Inquirer* (Budd was certain her missive was for him). That she should subsequently show her interest in a rather more intimate manner than did the map seller was not, perhaps, due entirely to her patriotism, but there can be no question that the Olympic mystique added considerably to my allure. I am ashamed I cannot remember her name.

Al gave us most of a week off after Amsterdam, and I went home to the farm for the first time in a year to be greeted with possessive pride by everyone who knew me even slightly. From the horsemen in the hunt country to the proprietor of the local gas station in Metamora, my hometown (population 600, about an hour north of Detroit), where gas sold for 29 cents a gallon, to the tellers at the bank—they all shared a bit of my Olympic dream although they had no idea what a rowing shell looked like. One man, Bill Queen, owner of a hunting stable and for whom I had particular regard, shook my hand on parting, a gesture of human communication we had not once indulged in during fifteen years of friendship, and told me to win the gold. Seriously. For some reason his uncharacteristic seriousness stayed with me and buoyed my determination throughout the competition. Another such parting came with my friend Tommy Charlton after a wild weekend in New York. My hero through the years since he had won his gold as captain of the Yale Crew in 1956 in Melbourne, Tommy saw me from his sister-in-law's Sutton Place apartment to my departure gate at Penn Central where, in his laconic way, he also wished me victory. He perhaps knew what I faced better than I, and his gesture in seeing me to the station, an unnecessary one I am sure he has forgotten, stayed with me.

Winning, as yet, was not much on my mind, even though it was the logical goal most mentioned by my well-wishers. They really had no notion what winning entailed. I was content then to work hard, harder during each workout, to concentrate within myself, to prepare with renewed fanaticism body and mind for what I imagined lay ahead. Time enough to worry about the hoopla of Tokyo, the excitement of the Games, to try to imagine racing two such magnificent crews as the Germans and the Soviets (which, unbidden, came often enough into the mind's eye). Time enough to get ready for that final "Etes vous prêts?" The psyching-up part I knew would take care of itself.

In the meantime, the idea was to get ready to go 2,000 meters at a 40 pulling as hard as I could. If I was going to lose—when I did slip up and imagine winning, it seemed, deep in the pit of my stomach, it would be impossible to beat either Ratzeburg or the Soviets—it was not going to be without a true Olympic effort, an effort for God and Country and Family and Bill Queen and Tommy, an effort I could live with for the rest of my life. There would be, win or lose, no repeat of the debacle on the Thames against Harvard in 1960. Notice I speak of "I," not "we." The whole effort was becoming even more personal. If there was any "we" it was me and Boyce; the others were just necessary—and eventually, as it always must, it turned out to be just me.

When we climbed back into the eight in August, Al put Boyce and me back at six and five where we belonged, moving Tom and Joe to the four and three seats. They bitched about it as they did everything not initiated by them, but as their place on the team was secure their complaints were more reflex than substantive. Eventually to separate them, to keep them from getting into each other's minds as they had in the pair, and to provide more power in the bow, Al moved Joe to the bow seat and Stanley down to three. That then was the final lineup from stern to bow; Zimonyi steering, Stowe at stroke, Knecht, 7; Budd, 6; Clark 5; T. Amlong, 4; Cwiklinski, 3; Foley, 2; J. Amlong, bow.

As the hot, languid days of August merged into the relative cool of September, we bore down, trying to knock tenths of seconds off our 500-meter times—1:21.8 was lots better than 1:22.2, and 1:23 was awful. The flat, tepid, dirty Schuylkill had almost no current, and as we fine-tuned, we each could tell within two-tenths of a second, and without Rosenberg's watch, what we had done. During the untimed hard strokes it was just a matter of never letting up, of exploding off each catch, of driving the boat through the water with the power in our legs, of trying to row harder on each stroke than the previous one even as we got more and more tired.

As the weeks dwindled to days before our departure, I could sense myself in pursuit of a dimly perceived ideal, a concept of perfection, separate from the competition, separate from winning. If I could close in on that ideal, if I could find it somewhere on the other side of the world on water I had never seen, then the winning would take care of itself. In the meantime, listen to Al, think in the boat, keep the blade buried at the finish, move the hands out of the bow smoothly and quickly, and pull harder on this stroke. It was all I could do and I was satisfied with it.

The morning workout before the heat of the day, always in the eight now, was usually free of distractions with only a few crews on the water. I was pleasantly conscious that the oarsmen in those other crews knew we were the Olympic eight. It was grand to be the undisputed king of the river, of all rivers, but the exigencies of the workout soon drove those self-con-gratulatory thoughts from a mind beginning to learn to concentrate.

The evening row, not leaving the dock until after six, was another matter. Then we would be accompanied by extra launches with visiting dignitaries, news reporters, coaches, and relatives. More than one car would follow the workout on East River Drive, in particular a little silver job containing a young lady known to me only as Legs, who it turns out

was pursuing the Big Budd, though he kept her well out of harm's way.

One afternoon, Joe Burk, from Penn next door, fitted each of our oarlocks with a preset stress gauge that measured the power in and during each stroke with the results shown on a panel of four lights down in the coxswain's seat. If you pulled hard in the first part of the stroke but eased off at the finish, only the first two of your four lights would come on. Your deficiency was there for all in the closely-following launch to see and for Robby to tell you about: "Tom, you're not pulling." As Tom Amlong's gauge, unbeknown to him or the rest of us, had been set fifty pounds heavier than the others by a mischievous Burk, it is small wonder he was savage by the end of a very bad and jerky workout. All of us were determined to light up our lights, caring nothing for the run of the boat, with Tom getting increasingly more vituperative as Robby continued to ride him: "Shut up. That fucking machine isn't working." Indeed, it was not.

The Olympic small boat trials in August produced predictable results with Conn, Ed, and Kent Mitchell winning the coxed pair at a walk, Tony

Philadelphia's Mayor James Tate wishing us well before we head off to Tokyo. Back Row, from left: Cwiklinski, Foley, Clark, Budd, J. Amlong, T. Amlong, Knecht, Stowe. Front Row, from left: Mayor Tate, Kelly, Doc Riggall (Vesper President for whom our boat was named), Rose, Rosenberg, Zimonyi

Johnson and Jim Edmonds taking the straight pair. Ted Nash and his college kids from the West Coast won in the straight four, while the middle four from the Harvard eight took the coxed four. Some weeks before we left, the two fours came down to Philadelphia to give us a race and to race themselves, as by that time most American oarsmen were winding down from a long summer of rowing. The Head of the Charles and the other head races[38] that are now fall classics and the highlight of many an oarsman's year were not even a gleam in the organizers' eyes.

I remember an easy if desultory win in the eight against the combined Olympic fours, a race in which I found myself fascinated with Teddy Nash's muscles. One can, and usually does, say what he likes about the gold medalist from Rusty Wailes' 1960 straight four in Rome, but Teddy was a hell of an oarsman—tough and competitive. But in a sport where there is no real premium on muscles—everybody's got them—Teddy, nonetheless, never wore a shirt unless the temperature was down around thirty-two degrees. Thus, it was easy for me paddling up to the start to watch the triceps pop out in Teddy's upper arm with each roll-up. I damn near pulled what muscles I had trying to emulate him, soon giving up this irreverent exercise as we set about to beat them. Teddy was an unlikely hero if one was anywhere near his age, not quite venerable enough.

The race against the coxed four, the hated Harvard coxed four, was another matter. With Robby steering, Tom Amlong stroking, me at three, and Boyce and Joe in the bow, I was going to be given two chances at beating Harvard in one summer. It did not matter that we were all Olympians now, all members of the same American team. The old wounds were healing, but there was still a scab to pick. It was only a race but they were still Harvard, still not talking to us (I expect we were unapproachably arrogant), still the Boston blue bloods.

Although we had not rowed the four for some time, we got out about a length on them in the first 30 strokes, took the rating down to 33 or 34

---

38 Generally these are three-mile races where crews start at 12-second intervals with the results determined by time.

Coach Allen Rosenberg (extreme left) with the Vesper Boat Club's eight-oared crew. Right to left, positioned as they are in the boat, are Coxsw
Zimonyi; Stowe, stroke; Knecht, No. 7; Tom Amlong, No. 6; Joe Amlong, No. 5; Budd, No. 4; Clark, No. 3; Foley, No. 2, and Cwiklinski, bow.

They're Ready for Tokyo

and watched them. We did not want to blow them away, yet. We wanted them to think they could move on us, but never let them; we wanted to keep contact and watch them work, strain, sweat. I felt no remorse. At the half-mile post, I looked out to port at Rosenberg and smiled. For some reason Al was not in the launch but was standing there on the bank with Ruth, the girl he would marry.

Coming into the last 500 at the head of the island with the finish 60 strokes away, the suppressed energy among the four of us was building to an intolerable level. We were itching to go, to crank it up to 38 or 40 and open up five lengths on them. Boyce grunted behind me, Tom cursed Robby telling him to call for three strokes to build it; but Robby, humanitarian that he was, countered with, "Vas de use, boys? Dey half to go." And he was right. They were the Olympic coxed four. They did have to go. It would only be destructive at this juncture to shatter their confidence, their self-esteem, to demonstrate they were but a poor second best in the United States. Tom swore some more, but the adrenalin subsided and we rowed on across the line still just a length ahead, and told them it had been a tough race.

For us there was satisfaction enough in knowing that among the four of us we had beaten three of the four sweep boats that would represent the United States in Tokyo that fall: the Amlongs had beaten Johnson and Edmonds in the straight pair at the Nationals, Boyce and I had done the same with Conn and Ed in the coxed pair,[39] and we had just demolished the Harvard coxed four. Heady stuff knowing we could have made the team in any of three boats in addition to the eight. The only Olympic crew we did not race was Teddy's straight four, but each of us was supremely confident we could have taken them, too. Three days in that boat to learn how to steer and there would have been no doubt…

If being a hero is, indeed, a function of others' perceptions, it carried with it certain social obligations I like to think we carried off with reasonable grace, as a crew and as individuals. At Al's request we rowed a demonstration at some fledgling boat club way upstream and attended a tea afterward. We graciously accepted a dinner at Philadelphia's famous Bookbinders (photo session with Kell and the owner afterward). We attended a B'nai Brith function at which Kell spoke. We were tested in a variety of ways at a sports medicine center at Valley Forge (the Amlongs were off all the charts and the rest of us were off most of them), and paraded at Eagles' football games where we passed the hat for amateur sport at halftime.

Indeed, we were so in demand that my sister, Carolyn, living then in nearby Wayne on the Main Line, reported to my mother in Michigan that we were doing more socializing than rowing. It didn't take her long to

Raising money
for Dietrich
Rose's trip
to Tokyo

39 I'm not at all sure we could have done it again.

VESPER BOAT CLUB

c/o JOHN B. KELLY, Inc.

1720 CHERRY STREET,   PHILADELPHIA 3, PA.

September 10, 1964

TO: ALL ROWING MEMBERS

FROM: JOHN B. KELLY, JR.

     The Vesper Boat Club has just completed the most successful season in its 99 year history. This was due to the tremendous efforts of a great many people – some of those who deserve particular recognition are Al Rosenberg, Dave Wilmerding, Joe Greipp, John McHugh and Deitrich Rose.

     We plan to have our annual Club Regatta on Sunday, September 20th, immediately following the Eagles football game. At this time we will christen the new shells purchased this year, particularly the two fours that have come from Italy. One will be named the "Paul Costello" and the other "Charles McIlvaine". We hope to have these two great Olympic Champions present with their families for this occasion. Informal races will be held among the squad and refreshments will be available.

     We will hold the Regatta after the Eagles Game for a special reason. We wish every possible Vesper oarsmen who can make it, to attend the Eagles-49er's Game to participate in an Olympic Parade just before kick-off, carrying the flags of approximately 100 nations. During the half the Vesper oarsmen and swimmers, along with some other A.A.U. athletes will take up a collection in the stands. Since we have had such success in placing oarsmen and swimmers on the Olympic Team – 16 in all – we have a great obligation to assist in this effort. We will be the guests of the Eagles for this Olympic Fund raising.

     Please return the enclosed card, indicating that we can count on your presence at twelve noon on September 20th on Weightman Hall steps. This is the building at the west end of Franklin Field. All members should wear blue jackets and gray trousers, if possible.

     If it were not for the fact that Deitrich Rose is not as yet an American citizen, he would have been on the squad going to the Tokyo Olympics. We had also hoped to have him included as assistant manager – this was not possible. We wanted Deitrich to go because we feel he is essential to rig our boats and to help Al Rosenberg with the coaching and training of the squad. His knowledge of international rowing is great and he provides a great inspirational force to the crew. For these reasons, I have made reservations for Deitrich to fly with the Olympic Squad, but it is necessary that we raise some money to help pay his fare. I am asking everyone who can afford it, to make out a check for as much as he possibly can, to the Vesper Boat Club, to help pay Deitrich's expenses to the Olympics. This also may be enclosed in the return envelope along with the card indicating whether or not you will be at the Eagles Game.

     A few who have not as yet paid their 1964 dues will find a bill enclosed. If you are not interested in rowing any longer, I would appreciate it if you would continue as a non-rowing member.

get her youngest son on the phone and explain to him her training rules, together with her firm expectation that we would win in Japan. Ma, as I knew her, could have been the commandant of the U.S. Marine Corps, and was, in today's parlance, a hard-ass. Naturally, I promised to pass her thoughts and feelings along. I shuddered to think of her encountering the Amlongs on one of their midnight beer drinking sprees.

About a week before we were to leave, the River Gods (or whatever deity makes sure human beings develop character) dropped a physical and emotional bomb in our midst as Boyce was diagnosed with mononucleosis. Being a hypochondriac myself (most world-class athletes are attuned to every nuance of their bodies), and having periodically suffered back problems that seemed certain to put me out of the boat, I knew what he was going through and was sympathetic. But not really. I was angry at him. Mad as hell. How could he? How could he, after coming this far, jeopardize the whole boat, the entire effort, my Olympic dream? For there was no question in my mind we could have substituted for anyone else in the boat, except Boyce. He just regularly pulled twice as much water as the rest of us, was twice as strong, had twice as much heart. I loved and love him. But I hated him then. The wolf-pack syndrome, when the pack turns on the wounded, took over. I wanted to kill him, but we needed Boyce, desperately, on any terms.

He must have suffered the tortures of the damned and almost certainly was not at full strength for the Games, but I wasn't much help to him, my single-minded purpose causing me to distance myself—so much so that after a year of having lived together we did not room together in Tokyo. The others were even less sympathetic than I, and the Amlongs, of course, were ruthless. All of us assumed his amorous liaison with "Legs" (he always kept her under wraps) was the cause, and I have no doubt that the insidious virus had a chilling effect on that romance.

In any case, he was out of the boat for nearly a week before we left, and it was only his terrific fitness and great strength that made it possible for him to come back when he did. That germ or virus or whatever it was bit off a big chew when it went after the Big Budd.

At long last our big adventure started at the Philadelphia airport sometime near the end of September. I think Doc Riggall, an old gent and longtime president of Vesper, was there to see us off. I had said good-bye to Gus Ignas, Don Horvat, Bobby Hardegan, Joe Burk, and the other regulars at Vesper. What a lot of fun we had had there! What a lot of good miles put in! A little sad. I knew I wouldn't be back. I burned my bridges. Out of the Marine Corps, without a job and footloose at age twenty-six, I had a plane ticket that went on round the world from Tokyo, so there was no sense kidding anybody. It was time to leave, too. I'm lucky it wasn't me that got mono. Strangely (irresponsibly), I had no particular anxiety about a life's work (i.e., job) or the lack thereof. Just as four years earlier I hadn't thought much beyond the Harvard race, now my focus didn't go much past that last "Partez!" and Ratzeburg.

CHAPTER 9

Los Angeles

BEFORE TOKYO, HOWEVER, THERE WAS ALL THE DISTRACTION and hoopla of Los Angeles. The entire U.S. Olympic Team assembled there to be outfitted and feted, and for the first time we came into contact with some of the nation's sports legends and athletes much better known than we were: Jesse Owens[40] was a fixture; Perry O'Brien, the shot-putter, there for his fourth Olympics; John Thomas, high jumper and first man to clear seven feet; Bob Hayes, the world's fastest human and future Dallas Cowboy wide receiver. It was fun living in the same hotel with the rest of the team, wondering in what sport the girl next to you at dinner excelled (I was usually too shy to ask) and what her chances were for the gold. That recurring thought, or perhaps obsession, was never far below the surface of my consciousness.

Some of the athletes were obviously old hands at representing their country, having competed in prior Games or the Pan Americans or on some world team. I envied them their apparent ability to relax and enjoy themselves in the face of the upcoming competition. Boyce and I, anyway, had a bit more of the country-boy-come-to-the-city-for-the-first-time mentality, but that wasn't bad either.

It was fun having everything paid for, too. Unlike some of the other athletes who had been training on Olympic Committee dollars for most of the summer, we had all been supporting ourselves up to that point—even

Mickey Mouse welcomes the 1964 Olympic team to Disneyland. Festivities included a parade in their honor, a steak dinner presided over by Walt Disney himself and entertainment by Bob Hope.

40 Hero of the '36 Games in Berlin and America's answer to Hitler.

though we had made the team in July. There is something deliciously sinful about getting things free, and Los Angeles was the place to indulge. I think you could have shown up there naked, without a toothbrush, and not had to buy anything for a year.

The uniforms, of course, were the first tangible evidence that we were Olympians. Most of us had dreamed a long time about wearing "USA" on our chests and having it mean what it meant here.[41] So it was with pride and not a little childlike glee that I collected my USA sweats and my workout uniform. Our racing colors, not to be worn until race day, were, I think, handed out later. Then came the number ones (dress uniform), the blue blazer Stowe was so looking forward to. Because President Lyndon Johnson was a Texan, our dress clothes, all made by Levi Strauss, had a western motif, topped off with an LBJ Stetson. It was hokey in a way, but we didn't mind. The clothes were irrelevant to our effort, part of the hype and good for trading. Although it was in great demand in Tokyo, for some reason I did not part with my Stetson. I have it still—kept it, I suppose, because I knew I was embarking on a once-in-a-lifetime fantasy and wanted to retain some of the trappings. I expect Cinderella pulled out her glass slipper every now and then in her maturity—not to try it on, just to remember.

The rest of the hype was pure Southern California. We paraded at Disneyland and got to go on all the rides free and bypassing the lines ("I don't give a goddamn who they are, I've been waiting in line an hour"). That afternoon was topped off by an outdoor steak dinner, hosted by no less than Walt Disney, with Bob Hope leading the entertainment. We marched in the L.A. Coliseum at halftime of a Rams football game. Everywhere we went, on display (the mayor of Los Angeles gave us each a medal) or otherwise, we were met with friendliness and warm good wishes. It is easy for Americans to be proud of and unselfish about their Olympic Team. In 1964 anyway, there was no controversy surrounding

---

41 When we raced in Amsterdam earlier that summer we sewed "USA" on a blue sweatshirt on the plane going over.

Dress uniforms for the opening and closing ceremonies were designed by Stetson and Levi Strauss with Texas president Lyndon Johnson in mind. Note Dietrich Rose on the far right.

the team. There would be no boycotts, no violence, no political statements. In what seems now like a kinder, simpler time, no one was looking for an international forum from which to voice his particular frustration.

Most on the team were young, healthy, fit, the best in America at what they did, and without commercial motive. It would be hard in any age not to be enchanted with our combination of youth and idealism. Avery Brundage's[42] unrelenting insistence on amateurism, while unrealistic and working individual injustices, had kept the profit motive at bay for most of the athletes. Amateurism in Brundage's sense of the word would eventually become unworkable, but in 1964 it was still in vogue and made the Olympic Team that much more appealing. Today, of course, most of the athletes are professionals, but somehow people still keep Olympians on a higher shelf in their hierarchy of values.

As for the amateurs in the Vesper eight, if we were innocent of the profit motive we were equally innocent of a media motive. Television, which had yet to adopt the Games as the huge profit-making venture that has become the financial backbone and an integral part of so much in American sports today, was the last thing on our minds. The press ignored us most of the time, and when it did appear, it was, from my conservative viewpoint, at obtrusive and inconvenient times—usually at some private moment in

42 President of the International Olympic Committee.

Posing for Royal Crown Cola was one of the duties that came with being an Olympian.

pre-race preparations. Like other ordinary prima donnas, we were hungry for the clippings afterward but did not go out of our way to help reporters make the news stories interesting or accurate. Rosenberg was an exception, but somehow they always wound up writing about Dietrich.

While it did not occur to me to "misbehave," whatever that meant (I was too single-minded, my soul too heavily burdened with the awesome task at hand), it occurred to others that I might. So we, the entire rowing team, were treated to what can only be described as a don't-do-anything-naughty-or-you-may-be-sent-home session with Rusty Wailes and John Sayre, two members of the gold medal straight four from the 1960 Rome Games. Rusty had won his first gold medal in the Yale eight in Melbourne in '56, and I had rowed with him in the '58 Yale varsity. I respected him enormously as an oarsman and human being but had little regard for him as my moral mentor. He had joined a quasi-religious international brotherhood called Moral Rearmament that I felt was exploiting him and turning him into a kook. His and Sayre's presentations were bland pablum delivered with great earnestness. Had I been prone to take it personally (it took me some time to figure out what they were driving at), I might have been offended at their demeaning presumptions. As it was, I was amused by the mentality of the blue-blazered fuddy-duddies who thought such drivel either necessary or effective. Imagine telling Stowe not to enjoy himself. I delighted in Joe Amlong, who undercut the entire be-good-boys speech by asking Rusty when he was going to start recruiting us for the brotherhood.

SEPTEMBER 25, 1964—California! Just lying here thinking of all the new impressions and thoughts that keep coursing through my head—seems like it would be awful easy to get caught up in the newness and the fun of the whole thing, and push the really serious business of the Germans and the Soviets into the background. But that is the realest reality. The meals are the most fun cause you sit next to a little black girl who can jump farther or run faster than anyone else in the world—or a swimmer or wrestler or boxer—and they all seem nice and most of them know the ropes having been to the Pan Ams or the World Championships somewhere. The workout wasn't bad, but it's a long way to Long Beach—three 500s which were fast cause the course was short—stiff wind and our boat doesn't like a wind—but I got up a sweat as well as a hard on for the Amlongs T and J who are both such numb nuts and refuse to shut up and leave Stowe alone and tend to their own rowing—yes, they got to me a little bit. Boyce is still nebulous but definitely does have mono—don't think he'll row till we get there, but I hope they don't give up on him—says he feels better.[43]

The workouts, in retrospect, were pretty miserable, although for obvious reasons we chose not to recognize it at the time. With Boyce still out of the boat, Tom Amlong moved from the four seat down to six, and Geoff Picard, stroke of the vanquished Harvard eight, got in at four. Naturally the boat didn't feel just right. But we did sweat, did our 500s, got in the work, which no doubt helped our minds more than our bodies. Three or four days out of sync, out of our two-a-day routine in our own

---

43 Started my journal again mostly to have someone (my inner self?) to confide in and redirect my angst with the Amlongs.

boat, away from our own boathouse on our own river, wasn't going to do our bodies much harm. But the mind that has nothing to occupy itself except for each nuance of each workout can be quickly affected.

We rowed out at Long Beach (nearly an hour from our L.A. hotel) in a borrowed Pocock. The course was salt water with cross breezes and currents and dozens of other insignificant differences that gave us an

UNITED STATES OLYMPIC TEAM
GAMES of the XVIII OLYMPIAD
Tokyo, Japan — October 10 - 24, 1964

INFORMATION FOR
PRESS · RADIO · TELEVISION

excuse for the boat being off, and an excuse not to think about being without Boyce. Picard, with whom I was to travel in Australia and who became a lifelong friend, did a fine job. He brought with him a different rowing style, philosophy, and tradition, and without much training (spares never get to train properly) stepped into the four seat without slowing us down appreciably. It must have been tough for him—just to do it and to row in the anything-but-gracious boat that had dashed his and Harvard's dreams three months before.

Official Press kit for the US Olympic Team.

About midway through our stay in Los Angeles, Boyce got back in the boat, to our great, if unexpressed, relief. He was scared mentally and weak physically (which put him about on a par with the rest of us), but Al told him to try it, to work back in slowly, and to signal the launch when he wanted Picard. We had done two or three 500s (with as many more to go) when Boyce started looking green around the gills (even from the back) and raised that huge right arm to wave at Al.

I think all my love and sympathy for Boyce were focused in that moment as I knew that was absolutely the last thing he wanted to do. One did not show weakness, ever, in that Vesper boat. There was nothing I could do or say, but that was never the case with Tom Amlong. Tom, who had moved grudgingly back to the four seat when Boyce returned, was wont to vent his finely tuned sensibilities at all opportune moments. So as the launch veered in toward our port side, we heard quite distinctly a low, guttural growl, "Fucking pussy." For a moment, as the back of Boyce's neck reddened and his muscles bunched, I thought he was coming over the top of me. When I turned to look at Tom, he showed his shark smile indicating how pleased he was to have caused the maximum amount of strife. Fortunately, the quest for the gold overrode even Tom's best efforts.

SEPTEMBER 28, 1964—Hard workout yesterday, if not so fast—two 500s with Boyce, two with Donovan and three miles at 31 with Picard. Boat not moving very well—Budd let Amlong get to him—box lunch at the course and then Disneyland—very well done there—lots of rides with no waiting and no paying—a fantastic dinner with the second steak better than the first, and the show with Bob Hope about as you'd expect, with two integration jokes the best, especially if you were sitting next to Erleen Brown (black shot putter, at 190 pounds)—hard to say what the average age of the team is as both extremes are well represented, but the crew seems fairly mature beside the swimming team, for instance, or the girls' volleyball—had a good close look at Rafer Johnson[44]—not as tall as I expected, but a rocky looking cuss. Packing up now.

NIGHT FLIGHT

Finally the stateside hoopla was finished, and with our new red, white, and blue suitcases packed with our new USA sweat suits and wearing our LBJ Stetsons, we boarded chartered jets for the long night flight to Tokyo. Beyond a refueling stop in Alaska, the flight was unremarkable—except for my traveling companion. I'm not sure why I was not sitting with someone from the crew. Perhaps I needed time with my own thoughts, or a respite from the ever-increasing pressure of the issue at hand—Ratzeburg. In any case, I couldn't have chosen a better seatmate, a medium-sized black athlete who did not appear disposed to conversation.

Why I felt I should bear that social responsibility, I don't know, but it was a long flight. So I asked him the obvious, "What sport?"—and he said, "Boxing," without elaborating. When I inquired as to what weight

44 1960 Olympic decathlon champion.

class, he replied, "Heavyweight." Then I bluntly asked what was really on my mind, realizing that I was not indulging in social amenities at all, but rather wanted to share my burden: "Do you think you're going to win?" It was then I got the slow, broad smile and Joe Frazier said to me, "I don't see any reason why not."

His response, which I found wonderfully simple yet compelling in its confidence, was so wildly at odds with the turmoil of doubt and fear and determination and pride that waged a constant battle in my breast that it stopped the conversation short. Here was an ego, a point of view that could occupy a few hours thought at 30,000 feet. Joe Frazier, who had battled his way out of South Carolina and the ghettos of North Philadelphia with his fists, was at the time just under six feet and 190 pounds. He had lost in the Olympic trials to a much larger man, Buster Mathis, but when Buster had broken his hand, Joe was chosen to fill in.

Possessed of a sunny disposition, a warm smile, and considerable charm, Joe was immediately popular in the Olympic Village, and more than once I saw him holding court with blond Scandinavian girls with whom I would no doubt have been tongue-tied. I was most envious of his unshakable faith in himself, however, and I had occasion in the weeks, days, and hours that led up to our races to contrast his self-confidence with my bouts of self-doubt. There is no question that as the determination to win battled with the spectre of Ratzeburg and the anticipation of the certain pain in the last 500 meters, I borrowed inspiration from Joe. His philosophy was physical. His right uppercut would resolve all outstanding questions.

I was lucky to get tickets to see his semifinal match against a big blond kid from the Ukraine. I went with my mother, whose philosophy of winning, while not quite as simple, was equally as indefatigable as Joe's. Her attitude toward any desired goal might be better described as implacable and no doubt had a great deal to do with her youngest son finding himself approaching that particular starting line. The Ukrainian tagged Joe solidly a couple of times in the first round, prompting Joe to step back, bow slightly, and smile, to the delight of the Japanese spectators. Then in the second round Joe stepped in and lifted the Ukrainian a half inch off the canvas with a thunderous right to the chin, and when the unhappy fighter struggled up, Joe dropped him again. That was when I first realized where the term "throw in the towel" came from, as the Soviet trainer, with a look of ultimate disgust on his face, took the towel off his shoulder and threw it into the ring, stopping the fight—no doubt saving his man from further battering. Smokin' Joe, as he was to become known later in his pro career, had a grand right hand.

Joe Frazier winning the gold against German mechanic Hans Huber, despite a broken thumb sustained in his semifinal match.

We couldn't get tickets to the final, so a group of us listened to the fight huddled around a radio. Joe was in against a big German who stood five inches taller than he, and the fight was lackluster from the beginning. The announcer kept saying, "Frazier with a left, Frazier ducks a punch, Frazier with another left," while we kept yelling at the radio, "Hit him with your right, Joe, hit him with your right." The German apparently never managed to land a solid blow, so Joe won his gold medal on points with his powerful left jab.

The next day in the Village, I came upon Frazier wearing a huge smile and a cast from the tips of his fingers to his elbow on his right arm.[45] It turned out he had broken his thumb fighting the Ukrainian but had wisely not told the powers-that-be in the blue blazers, knowing he would not be permitted to fight, and that he would be denied his chance for the gold. So he won his medal with one hand and courage and that wonderful faith in himself. Along the way he lent some courage and faith to an itinerant oarsman who he happened to sit next to on a plane.

---

45 My sure memory always summons up Joe's right arm in the cast. Yet even Joe himself in his book, "Smokin' Joe", indicates it was his left arm, his left thumb the one broken. Right or left, it doesn't matter to me. Joe won the gold with one hand—and will always be my Olympic hero.

CHAPTER 10

Japan

AFTER HAVING SPENT THIRTEEN MONTHS IN THE ORIENT with the Marines, my return to Japan was not accompanied with the first-time wonder most Westerners feel on landing in Tokyo. I was by no means an expert, even though I had experienced the glitter of the Ginza, been put up in Frank Lloyd Wright's Imperial Hotel, seen the cherry blossoms, and slept under the stars on Mount Fuji's comfortable bosom. But I was not engulfed by the exquisite strangeness that comes with experiencing a rich culture foreign in every aspect from our own. Most Americans can sense their roots, or at least some foretaste of their culture, on a trip to Europe. Not so in Japan.

SEPTEMBER 30, 1964—And we lost a day coming over—not a bad flight—got a fair bit of sleep. Stopped in Anchorage and got in at 6:00 a.m. Japan time. Sat next to Joe Frazier, our heavyweight boxer. Yesterday, before catching the plane, we went to the L.A. Athletic Club to work out but wound up just sitting in steam for a few minutes and weighing ourselves—me at 207, Boyce 212; bet the boat is 50 lbs. heavy. Had my shoes dyed, changed some money, got a haircut, called home and Suzy.

Looks like a pretty good set-up here—drew our rowing gear today (sweat suit too small) and got our old boat (flown over from Vesper) rigged (new eight not in sight, although all the new Pocock small boats are here). Rowed about 2000 meters at dark and it felt good, real good. Ready to go to work. Rumors already flying—German stroke sick, etc. See Cuba and Korea have eights here. Olympic Village looks like it might be fun—after we finish—good chow, eating with Great Britain mainly—unpacked now and in the sack.

In one sense, of course, it didn't matter where we rowed. We were prepared to go to the ends of the earth, the Arctic Sea or the Gulf of Siam, to race the Germans.

It turned out the Olympic Games could not have found a better host country. Less than twenty years gone from its devastating defeat and General MacArthur's occupation after World War II, Japan had risen from the atomic ashes and was ready to show the world it was a thriving, modern, democratic nation. The Games were its first opportunity to focus positive international attention on itself, to invite the rest of the world in, and to show heartfelt and open hospitality.

And, as the athletes experienced it, that hospitality was ubiquitous. If there were dissidents, student protesters, anti-Olympic factions, or terrorists looking for a forum, they were nowhere apparent. Nor was there a sense that the Japanese were hiding or covering up anything. Unlike the 1980 Moscow Olympics where the Soviets were said to have shipped the schoolchildren out of town so they would not be contaminated by the foreigners, the Japanese shipped theirs in, reserving perhaps ten thousand seats in the Olympic Stadium each day for them—obvious in their neat, dark uniforms.

The Japanese government, the nation's industrial and commercial sectors, and, indeed, the people as a whole all joined to welcome us and cater to every possible wish. We were showered with gifts (presentos) of cosmetics and fans and flags and souvenirs by the Japanese retailers. There were free passes on Japanese railroads, official coin sets, and participation medals (we thought they were fine for the losers). Children from all over Japan made traditional dolls, whose significance went back

Oct. 21—25

Meal Coupon
for Athletes and Officials

TEAM

NAME

TOKYO 1964 GAMES OF THE XVIII OLYMPIAD

OLYMPIC VILLAGE

TOKYO 1964

Oct. 24 1964

朝食

Breakfast
Déjeuner

Oct. 22 1964

夕食

Dinner
Dîner

Oct. 22 1964

昼食

Lunch
Déjeuner

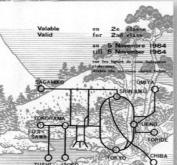

CONDITIONS D'UTILISATION

(1) Le titulaire de cette carte de circulation doit, quand il fait son usage, porter sa Carte d'Identité.
(2) Cette carte n'est valable que sur les lignes de zone indiquées dans le schéma ci-contre.
(3) Cette carte n'est valable que pour les trains omnibus.
(4) Cette carte ne sera pas délivrée à nouveau en cas de perte.

INSTRUCTIONS

(1) The user of this pass must carry his Identity Card.
(2) This pass is valid for travel within the sections shown in the drawing.
(3) This pass is good for local trains only.
(4) This pass shall not be re-issued.

Valable   en   2e   classe
Valid   for   2nd class

au   5 Novembre 1964
till 5 November 1964

sur les lignes de zone indiquées ci-dessous.
within the section shown below.

SAGAMIKO   OMIYA
SHINJUKU
YOKOHAMA   UENO
FUJI   TORIDE
SAWA
ZUSHI ISOGO TOKYO CHIBA

日本國有鉄道

鐵道乗車證

CARTE DE CIRCULATION

RAILWAY PASS

TOKYO 1964

東京都区内私鉄優待乗車証
FREE PASS FOR PRIVATE RAILWAY LINES
IN TOKYO AREA

1. 持参人 1名
   Good for : Holder only.
2. 有効区間 裏面表示の赤網区間
   Lines available : Lines indicated in red ink.
   (See the reverse side map)
3. 有効期間 昭和39年9月25日~11月5日
   Period : September 25~November 5 1964

東京私鉄協議連合会
Liaison Council of Private Railways in Tokyo

TOKYO 1964

No 006579

Tokyo memorabilia: meal tickets, a railway
pass, and commemorative stamps.

Olympic Village from the air with swimming and basketball venues in the foreground.

centuries, which were presented to every athlete. When Don Schollander, the young, blond American swimmer from Yale who won four gold medals in the pool, left for home, there was a room filled literally from floor to ceiling with presents he was unable to take with him, or even unwrap. The whole country seemed Olympics-mad. In reality, retailers, who had counted on a bonanza from the influx of foreigners, were sorely disappointed because whenever the competitions were underway the visitors were watching, not in the stores buying.

Nor was the Japanese hospitality merely general; it extended to the specific. For years I have pondered how the organizers knew there would be a six-foot-four athlete sleeping in a certain bed on a certain floor in a certain building in the Olympic Village. But less than a half-hour after we arrived in our rooms on the third or fourth floor of what was a Bachelor Officers' Quarters (BOQ) on the Army base that comprised the Village, a little Japanese man appeared asking me in broken English and sign language if I would like an extension on my bed. A short while later my bed was two feet longer, and if I did not sleep soundly in the days leading up to the races, it was not because the Japanese did not do everything they could to make sleep possible.

Because the U.S. and Soviet delegations were the largest, they were

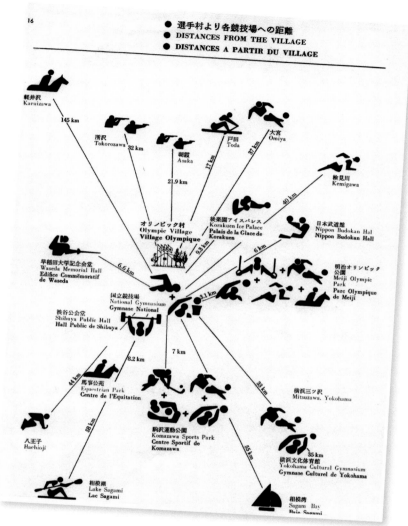

16

● 選手村より各競技場への距離
● DISTANCES FROM THE VILLAGE
● DISTANCES A PARTIR DU VILLAGE

軽井沢
Karuizawa

145 km

所沢
Tokorozawa 32 km

朝霞
Asaka

21.9 km

戸田
Toda

17 km

大宮
Omiya

37 km

検見川
Kemigawa

40 km

オリンピック村
Olympic Village
Village Olympique

後楽園アイススケート
Korakuen Ice Palace
Palais de la Glace de
Korakuen

9.3 km

日本武道館
Nippon Budokan Hall
Nippon Budokan Hall

6 km

早稲田大学記念会堂
Waseda Memorial Hall
Edifice Commémoratif
de Waseda

6.6 km

明治オリンピック
公園
Meiji Olympic
Park
Parc Olympique
de Meiji

国立競技場
National Gymnasium
Gymnase National

3.1 km

渋谷公会堂
Shibuya Public Hall
Hall Public de Shibuya

7 km

8.2 km

馬事公苑
Equestrian Park
Centre de l'Equitation

44 km

58 km

横浜三ッ沢
Mitsuzawa, Yokohama

33 km

八王子
Hachioji

駒沢運動公園
Komazawa Sports Park
Centre Sportif de
Komazawa

55 km

35 km

横浜文化体育館
Yokohama Cultural Gymnasium
Gymnase Culturel de Yokohama

相模湖
Lake Sagami
Lac Sagami

相模湾
Sagam Bay
Baie Sagami

Drawing of event venues and their distances from the Olympic Village showing the Toda rowing course a mere 17km (about 10.5 miles) away. But it took nearly an hour to get there through Tokyo traffic even with a motorcycle escort with flashing lights leading the way.

housed right next to each other in two BOQs, while the smaller teams were scattered about the base in the housing intended for married officers with families. The women were segregated, indeed fenced off, from the rest of the Olympic Village, and heavily chaperoned. The idea of a little casual sex between young, healthy athletes was not something that stuffy old fuddy-duddies could begin to contemplate.

Notwithstanding the fuddy-duddies, sex was never far from anyone's mind and the Amlongs still talked about it, or the lack of it. But with a fast-approaching starting line, it was reasonably easy to relegate it to a secondary position. We did flirt, however.

Olga Connolly, Czechoslovakian gold medalist in the discus in Melbourne, had married American hammer throw gold medalist Harold Connolly and was competing as an American in her third Olympics. She cared nothing for the fuddy-duddies and was determined to eat with her husband in the men's dining room if and when she chose. A large (six-foot-two), well proportioned, handsome woman, I was awed by her and ate as close to her as I could (always wary of the sometimes-glowering Harold). Happy to be in her energy field, to feel the force of her personality, I was, I suppose, hoping some of whatever had made her a gold medalist would rub off on me. Her principal competition, the U.S.S.R.'s Tamara Press, also managed to ignore the fence, but her focus was rather the weight-lifting apparatus the Soviets had set up outside their barracks. We used to watch Tamara bench pressing 250 pounds, bouncing the bar off her chest, and we experienced a different kind of awe. Tamara, who would win the gold in both the shot put and the discus, was neither handsome nor well proportioned.

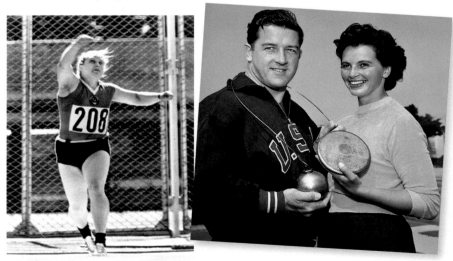

USSR shot-putter Tamara Press was impressive on the field but lacked the charisma and back-story of USA team members Harold and Olga Connolly.

Security at the Olympic Village was tight with only one way in and out, not so much because of terrorists' threats or fear of violence, but rather more innocently to shield the athletes from the public and press. The main entrance was well staffed with Japanese women dispensing information and directions, while others acted as interpreters for every language represented in the Games. I made friends with the French interpreters and would stop by their booth every day on the way to and from the race course to practice my schoolboy French. I have found in various countries around the world it is easier to speak French with persons for whom it is a second language rather than with native Frenchmen. Anyway, I enjoyed my daily visits with the Japanese women, and, after the regatta, about which they were intensely interested, I was able to get them autographs of everyone in the crew. If we collected souvenirs of our storybook time in Japan, the Japanese were equally assiduous in collecting memorabilia of our visit.

One thing you could not take out the front gate was the bicycle, which was the Japanese's rather ingenious method for getting around the sprawling Olympic Village. I don't know how many thousand bikes were provided, but the idea was that you simply found a bike and rode it to your destination where you left it, presumably for someone who wanted to go in the other direction. That worked fine, except when it was raining (which it did a lot), or when everyone wanted to go in the same direction at the same time. I don't know what those of us did who never learned to ride a bike.

One common destination was the dining halls, which were centrally located and where we ate morning and night. There were a whole series of kitchens, each specializing in the cuisines of the athletes from the competing nations. The Japanese imported cooks from around the world to make sure each athlete had the opportunity to eat something he recognized (steak and French fries in our case). We dined with the English and the Canadians, and, as sports' nutrition was not yet a well-developed science, were served traditional meat-and-potatoes meals, although we

The French interpreters booth in the Olympic village was a favorite stop.

had a choice of Japanese fare as well. The French and Italians ate in the dining room next to ours, and I couldn't help wonder at the bottles of wine that were a fixture on their tables. Beer was one thing, but somehow that wine tended to make me discount their speed.

The Toda rowing course, running parallel to the Toda River, was about an hour out of Tokyo. Seven lanes wide with the boathouse off the finish, the course was protected by sloping banks that absorbed a good deal of the wash from the launches and was generally fair, although like any course, a strong side or quartering headwind could mess things up pretty badly. Built by the Japanese for the 1940 Olympics, its original purpose was thwarted by world war. In retrospect, there seems considerable historical irony in meeting the Soviets and Germans on this 2,000-meter bathtub in the heart of Japan, but it was lost on me at the time. As I said, I didn't care or think much about where I rowed. I wanted to go to whatever finish line at which they handed out gold medals and played "The Star-Spangled Banner."

OCTOBER 2, 1964—I get so pissed off I can't see straight—going to be a tough life if I let things get to me the way they are here. So our manager is a numb nuts and couldn't be more incompetent; so Al is nebulous and inconsistent; so nobody pulls—Jesus! I've gotten to thinking that about half the boat isn't pulling—can you imagine?! In the Olympic eight! Nine miles this morning in rotten water and no power—crosstail wind. But now I think I'm better than everyone else—that's a hell of a way to be at a time like this.

But no one wants to hurt themselves—just figuring they'll do it when the chips are down—I think you got to do it in practice—Boyce looked like he was pulling about half what he used to—Knecht, I don't know—doubts—terrible—two 500s this afternoon 1:23.5 and 1:25—slow for the conditions, but I'm not too worried about actual speed—Aussies picked us up for 30 strokes—held them okay, but didn't move. When I think how fast we go and how fast we could go it makes me want to cry.

I just get savage thinking about all the little things that aren't being done. They piss me off not because they themselves are so important, but just because the people who should care don't seem to. Wish I could not sweat it like Knecht. But I guess I'm a congenital sweater. At times today I could see us not making the finals, let alone beating anybody—was going to write Suzy but had nothing very good to say—one of those nights when you feel like the only thing you can do is go to bed and sleep—tomorrow it ought to look up. Even writing in the journal doesn't help, but one good row and none of this petty stuff will bother me.

We went out to the course every morning on the bus and stayed all day. A mini-controversy, which was never resolved, immediately became apparent there. Unlike the Germans and other Western athletes used to beds and toilets, and so placed, we were billeted in Japanese-style quarters in a room with nothing but tatami mats[46] and futons on the floor. Further, the bathrooms were Oriental style—ceramic holes in the floor for toilets, and no handrails. Easy enough to manage for Asian folks used to squatting on their heels when doing their business, but awkward to cope with for hulking Americans. Emptying out before a workout, or, more important, a race was a significant part of every oarsman's pre-row ritual. As we were all prima donnas strung as tight as the E string on a violin,

---

46 Type of mat made of rice straw with a covering of soft woven rushes used as flooring in traditional Japanese rooms.

The Amlongs (Joe left) with USSR sculler, Ivanov, and his coach.

any little change from the norm or apparent ill treatment was blown out of proportion. When we found out the Germans had arranged for hot lunches, while we ate sandwiches and cold cuts, we were particularly irate. It was illogical to be billeted as we were, but to the Japanese's credit, it was not their doing. The FISA regatta committee was responsible for who got what at the race course.

It was our manager who dropped the ball, using neither foresight, ingenuity, nor diplomacy. In fact, the main man, from the Detroit Boat Club, who shall remain nameless, was worthless on the trip, which for him was really a reward for polishing the proper apples in the four years prior to the Games. His principal goal was to get his international referee's license so he could wear his blazer all the time. (So much for subjective opinion.)

Prima donnas though we were, we put up with our quarters with considerable good grace accompanied by considerable sarcastic humor. Our bigger and more serious problem was our wet gear. Given the constant rain and ordinary sweat, our rowing stuff was always sopping. We did not have enough changes. We started getting serious colds—one of the fellows in Teddy Nash's four got so sick he couldn't race. Needless to say, that kind of thing is not conducive to calm or concentration when you are preparing for the ultimate test in your young life. (Could there, indeed, be life after the Olympics?)

I got so mad one evening back at the Village I gathered up everybody's wet clothes and dumped them outside the team manager's door just as he was emerging. Dressed to the nines in his Olympic blazer dripping with national pins, he announced he was on his way to a party in downtown Tokyo and thus really would not have time to deal with the soggy, smelly pile of clothes, which he stepped gingerly around. The same man had the effrontery to ask me when our first heat was when he theoretically was the manager. In retrospect, it was probably good to have someone nonessential to our effort who we could be mad at all the time.

So, thank God for Dietrich. He provided the glue that held us together and was the actual, if unofficial, manager for our eight. I don't remember how he got to Tokyo, but I know Vesper (Kelly) paid his way and got him official credentials. It was Kell who had the good sense to understand we needed a person who knew rowing at the elite level, was an

Practice on the Toda race course where we honed our stroke working to find the racer's edge.

old hand at international regattas, someone, further, who was unselfish, whose ego never overrode the eight's best interest.

Rosenberg was a genius as a coach—at least for our boat—but, despite his antipathy for sharing the limelight, he needed considerable logistical shoring up. And Dietrich was there, arranging for the bus or lunch or fixing a slide or tightening a rigger bolt. In fact, Al disappeared for a while after we got to Tokyo. I think he was getting a hernia fixed for free by the U.S. team doctors. Dietrich acquired a motor scooter from somewhere and ran the workouts from the towpath. Not that we needed much coaching then; the die was pretty well cast and the workouts fixed, so many 500s or so many hard strokes. But even though we knew the workouts, we needed that voice through the megaphone giving us something to think about, focusing our concentration. We needed a hand to hold the watch, a friend to tell us our split, to let us know we were coming back into top form, that we could move a boat on the far side of the world.

OCTOBER 4, 1964—I don't think I've been so pissed off at anyone since I contemplated drowning Robert Felheim in the rapids somewhere in Quebec when I was 16. Yes, Tom really got to me yesterday and murder wasn't good enough— only torture of the most painful variety would suffice.

We picked up a little yesterday morning doing four 500s. About 30 strokes with the Arabs and they had to go high to stay with us. Was a beautiful day with good water—figure we were maybe a second slow in the first three and might have hit 1:20 if we'd pushed it. Ivanov's[47] coach got our second 500 at 1.22 so they know we're within striking distance. Then in the afternoon we rowed the new boat.[48] Seemed like we were rigged too low and felt loggey with Amlong mouthing off constantly. In any case the lift

47 Great Russian single sculler who beat Kelly in '56 in Melbourne and would win his third Olympic gold in Tokyo.
48 A Donoratico, just arrived from Italy.

of the morning was shattered by the afternoon and, as Robby said, everyone seemed somewhat somber—mostly disgusted with Tom.

Today Stan is sick with a cold or virus or something and Chet[49] will row in his place. My attitude hits the extremes regularly—sometimes I think we're going to blow it like the Philadelphia Phillies,[50] and other times I think we're going to be in there. As Foley said, it's "agony" to row with Tom. I guess I'm too sensitive—but it doesn't seem like what an Olympic effort ought to be. At times it's almost a physical thing—this agony Hugh is talking of—gives me a headache, and the only cure is sleep because my thoughts are too unkind, but it's impossible to concentrate on anything else. Oh well, the idea now is to keep my mouth shut, do my best, not let it get to me, pray...

Thank God for the workouts—the reassurance of the oar handle. After all the strangeness and wonder and distraction of the flight, the city of Tokyo, the Olympic Village, and the other athletes, to grip the oar handle again was a profound relief. That was the one thing that we knew. If we could concentrate on a stroke we didn't have to think, to doubt, to wonder, to fantasize, to fear. With the oar in our hands, destiny was ours. It alone channeled the fierceness of our desire, the intensity of our spirit. It was grand to get back in the boat.

But, of course, we had to share the race course. I believe there were twenty-eight nations competing in the regatta, fourteen of which had sent eights. And as we all came out in the morning from the Olympic Village, we were all on the course at more or less the same time—except for the Soviet eight. Those guys rowed only once a day, usually while the rest of us were sleeping (attempting to sleep on our tatami mats). I don't know if the Soviets were trying to hide something, but they had intimidated me way back in Amsterdam in their magnificent race against the

49 Chet Riley, our starboard spare.
50 The Phillies had a six-game lead in the National League when we left for Tokyo and blew it by the end of September.

Germans, so out of sight was definitely not out of mind. Mine anyway. As for the rest of the crews, I tried not to notice.

OCTOBER 5, 1964—Another nice day and only one workout—lots of people in attendance. Ivanov's coach was explaining to Tom that I didn't go far enough up my slide at the catch before we went out; and the U.S. rowing officials showed up as well as Armed Services' reporters.

In the new boat with Chet at three, we took five slow 500s and did some no slide work. It was almost bliss, though, as Tom didn't say anything and Al coached us for the first time. Everyone worked and even though it was slow we came in optimistic. Chet did a good job—boat was still sluggish but set up better. Think Dietrich is going to lighten the load[51] today.

The Danes and the Swiss showed up and I saw my friends from the Swiss straight pair. Got our pins,[52] but the market is so glutted now no one wants to trade for an American pin—bucket of worms—guess I'll have to give them away to deserving people. Signed up for tickets to events after our competition. Looks windy today.

Was windy—a strong crosswind from the starboard side—three 500s up the course, two down, couldn't seem to handle the latter at all but three up were solid and sharp with the load on the oars considerably lighter. Last one felt particularly good at 1:21. Germans were clocked at 1:21 today, too, so we can't be too far off the pace. Somehow I get the feeling they are about 2 to 3 seconds faster than we are over the distance, but on the other hand, I just don't think we are going to lose. But, if the Germans are half a second faster over 500—as the rumors (for what they're worth) indicate—then so are the Soviets, and the Czechs. Most observers put us in the finals with a decent chance in a little headwind.

51 Move the buttons down the oars; less or more leverage; a centimeter makes a difference.
52 I think the USOC issued each of us fifty USA lapel pins.

Stan was in the hospital today, but Chet did a good job. It's amazing, but no one (if they're like me) seems worried about it, I guess figuring Chet is just as good a man. Not at all like when Boyce was ailing.

We marched in a welcoming ceremony this afternoon, me in the second row next to John Thomas (high jump) and behind four of the biggest bastards I've ever seen in my life, all on the basketball team and averaging 6'11". Went to watch the swim team work out tonight—the pool is just amazing, sort of like the Yale hockey rink, but ever so much bigger and more intricate, labyrinthian really, with great sweeping, thrusting lines, powerful in effect and not symmetrical. Beginning to get a cold. Hope the wind dies.

Ratzeburg was awesome. I have a vivid memory of the Yugoslav eight taking off, short and without splash, at what I thought was a paddle but by the sixth stroke realized was the smoothest racing start I'd ever seen. I was not aware of the Czechs until they lined up next to us in the final. Our isolation in North America probably helped, as we rarely knew who we were looking at anyway, and that ignorance allowed us to concentrate in our boat.

There was enough to keep us occupied. Boyce was back in the boat, but still hurting and doubting himself. Instead of pulling half again as much water as the rest of us, his puddle was much closer to being human. We all got more or less sick in the rain and cold, but Stan got sicker than the rest of us and was out for a while, with Chet Riley filling in. I tried to tell myself Chet was just as good, and perhaps he was, but I didn't believe it. And as the competition grew closer and our nerves stretched tighter, the aggravation that the Amlongs caused seemed to intensify.

One morning at the dock as we were going out, they showed up with the coach of the Russian sculler, Ivanov. He began explaining by gesture (pointing at me sitting in the five seat) and broken English that the break in the boat, the reason we were slow, was because my shins were not perpendicular to the bottom of the boat when I was at the catch. An accurate enough observation, but one apparently having little to do with our speed. Rather it was all part of the constant psyche game that was played on and off the water. If ever there were two fellows susceptible to it they were Tom and Joe—head cases. They played mind games with themselves and the rest of us and psyched themselves out in the process.

But by that time the rest of us weren't much better. Every time we took off on a piece there were ten or twelve stopwatches on us: six Japanese, two Soviet, two Germans, and so on. To throw them off we would start a 500-meter piece at the 1,100-meter mark and row to the 1,600 or at the 400 and go to the 900. After the first week, we knew the Germans (Dietrich was our spy) were consistently a half second faster than we were in their 500-meter splits (1:21:2 to our 1:21:7). It was not hard to put four half seconds together and imagine ourselves two seconds, or half a length down at the finish. I was never a whiz at math, but that was one bit of arithmetic I could not stop myself from doing, with the same result each time.

OCTOBER 6, 1964—Rumors were rife today. Russians rowed a 5:55, the Canadians 6:06, and the Aussies 6:08 over the course. We took six 500s with Chet still at 3. Boat was moving except for the middle two. Cleaned Teddy[53] and his four in the last two after he'd been obnoxious in the previous two.

The heats came out at noon and we drew Ratzeburg, Italy, Yugoslavia and Australia for what has to be the toughest heat. Took a while to adjust to getting the Germans, but the odds were for either them or the Russians, who got all the patsies (Japan, Korea). Took 1,000 with the Aussies this afternoon and after a bad start (dropped two seats and sat awhile) managed to get almost a length on them in 3:01. Not a bad time in a decent head wind. Then one more 500 in 1:24 (tailwind). Amlong mouthing off again. But a good day on the whole—things looking up. Met the Russian bow, three and stroke tonight at

---

53 Ted Nash and the American straight four.

the International Club—stroke is a little bastard—compared times, etc. They wanted to know by how much we beat Harvard. Seem like nice guys. Stan back in the boat tonight.

The workouts were the only relief, and I found myself getting fiercer and fiercer as I attacked the water with the oar handle on each, now precious, stroke. Time—before that final, heart-stopping *"êtes vous prêts"*—was running out. And while I had been dreaming of that moment for the last thirteen months, now it was upon me. I wanted to savor it a while. I was strong. I was fit, mean fit. I felt I would never be in that kind of shape again (veterans' rowing did not exist). My spirit was ready to be tested. I had spent three years bleeding internally since running the gauntlet of that Harvard-Yale finish line, and then thirteen months ensuring I would never again suffer such a crisis of courage—for that is how I saw that long-ago Harvard race.

I was primed for an Olympic effort. And as I watched Boyce's puddle and heard Stan cough and listened to the Amlongs bicker and worried about Allen's insecurities, I somehow felt I was the strength in the boat, I had to do it all, *was* doing it all—which is ridiculous in an eight. But maybe it was good that I felt that way. Rowing in an eight is ultimately an individual experience.

OCTOBER 7, 1964—Just back from the Ambassador's (Edwin O. Reischauer) party for the Olympic Team where I fell in love (sigh)—her name is Lesley and she's sixteen (can you beat that?), and she's blond and a diver and she figures to win a gold medal. Oh well.

We did five 500s this morning and four this afternoon, splitting them up between Stan and Chet in the three seat—not fast, not slow—Al says we're better than the Germans by 1.5 seconds over the course. I'm for that. Al's full of bullshit. Felt good physically. Chet's stronger, Stan's timing is better. Going to have to go with one or the other pretty soon—have confidence in both—too late to worry.

We carried the boat over to the Toda River one day where Al had lined up a launch. The idea was to get off by ourselves on some water where we could go more than 2,000 meters. It was exhilarating being free of the confinement of the lane markers, the constriction of starting and finish lines. Perhaps, for those reasons, our starts were fabulous—clean, sharp, powerful, fast. Al clocked us at least once at a 52. We were flying and knew if we could do that in the race nobody would beat us off the line. If…

OCTOBER 8, 1964—Rain, rain, rain—carried the boat over to the river and took 400 hard strokes—Stan back in—it was real good— easy to set up and I'm really getting it on. Two good starts at a 50. Began picking up my pre-race aches today—the old one in the lower back that I had before the trials—just an ache that makes it so you can't lie on your back and catches you when you don't expect it, then a new one in the right shoulder, a muscle pain that I guess I'll ignore.

We took two not so good 500s on the course tonight and called it a soggy day. Ate dinner with Olga Connelly[54]—a magnificent woman. She told us about meeting Bob Hope (hypocrite) in Paris and how screwed up the American Team administration always is. Talked to Geoff Picard (Harvard stroke) tonight about rowing together in Australia after the Games. Seems like a nice guy.

Back in the Village we quickly adapted to the routine. It didn't seem strange anymore to wear our USA sweats all day. Everyone wore them. We were no longer awed by magnificent physiques. I stopped wondering if the huge man walking by with CCCP on his chest was the five man in the Soviet eight. Everybody had muscles. What mattered was what you could do with them.

54 As noted above, Olga refused to follow the rules and ate with the men—and her husband, Harold Connelly, American hammer throw champion. A discus thrower, after winning the gold medal for Czechoslovakia in the '56 Games, she competed in four Olympics for the United States, carrying the flag in Munich in '72.

One man I saw who knew what to do with them was Al Oerter, the American discus thrower. I was in the U.S. infirmary, for a head cold I think, when they were working on Oerter who had apparently just ripped the muscles off his rib cage—and awesome muscles they were (Ted Nash notwithstanding). They shot him full of cortisone and Novocain, taped him up, and told him not to practice anymore. It became obvious he did not need more as three days later he won his third Olympic gold with a world-record throw.

It got harder and harder for me to sleep as the start of the Games approached. The insomnia that had dogged me through the rowing seasons at Yale came back to haunt me.

Among other things, I dreamed about Tom Amlong at night, and in that shadow world between wakefulness and sleep I fantasized about killing him. Seriously. But then I decided if I ever tried it he would kill me instead. So the fantasy switched to Tom chained to a wall (legs and arms) with me beating him senseless with some sort of blunt instrument. Clearly Tom got under my skin. The image of him at the wall (it was whitewashed stone) is vivid still. All of this mayhem, of course, was to take place after the regatta. We needed Tom to beat the Germans.

Other than eating, trying to sleep, and taking the bus to and from the rowing course, we did not do much in the days leading up to the regatta. My parents and my sister Carolyn came from the States, and my brother, Bill, came over from Korea where he was an Army flight surgeon. It was nice to know they were there, I had gotten over the anxiety of my college days when I wanted everyone to stay away, but I didn't need to see them much before the races. In any case, they decided young Emory had better concentrate and commune (Yale style) with the others in the boat. They wouldn't have believed me if I had told them I wanted to kill Tom and was mad at everyone else.

Soon after our arrival we attended a reception given by the U.S. ambassador to Japan. I recall little except wearing our blazers and falling in love with Lesley Bush, a little American diver from Princeton who was

Crowds outside the Olympic Village were always eager for autographs, and always hoping for one from a famous athlete.

to win the first gold medal for the United States in the Games. The steel fence in the Village and my general inarticulateness made short shrift of romance—that and the fact that at sixteen Lesley was ten years my junior.

When we were bored or wanted an ego boost, we could step out the front gate of the Village and sign autographs for the constant crowd assembled there. For the big-name athletes, autographs were a chore, but for us common garden-variety Olympians it was something of a thrill and an exercise most of us suspected would not trouble our later years.

I indulged in that pleasant pastime on several occasions, signing programs and napkins and bits of paper taken from dozens of eagerly outstretched hands. At first I wrote my name and "U.S. Rowing Team" or "U.S. Olympic Eight-Oared Crew" or some such. However, I soon switched to a bit of lighthearted fraud and misrepresentation. After watching the proud possessors of my penmanship rush back to their friends, then seeing their faces fall when they realized the tall, light-haired American was a no-name in an esoteric sport, I decided to do better. I started signing "Al Oerter" or "Don Schollander" or "Bill Bradley."[55] This innocent subterfuge produced instant and happy results, as these athletes were much in the headlines, and if my ego suffered somewhat, it was nothing I could not sustain. I was more than happy to be simply an American Olympian.

55 Princeton basketball player who later starred for the New York Knicks, and still later was a Democratic senator from New Jersey and a presidential candidate.

CHAPTER 11

Opening Ceremonies

THE OPENING CEREMONIES WERE SPECTACULAR and provided a welcome respite from the concentration on and growing pressure of the now inevitable regatta.

Not a show or an extravaganza choreographed for a worldwide television audience, these ceremonies were just that, the dignified opening of the Games—filled, nonetheless, with color and pageantry, music, and emotion, the last supplied by the athletes, the audience, and the interaction between them.

Being less than six months out of the Marine Corps, where parades are conducted with sharpness and precision, I was taken aback by the sloppiness and informality with which we formed up and waited, dressed in our blazers and Stetsons, for the march into the stadium. After some reflection I realized why. We were all intensely individualistic in our various quests, and the only discipline most of us recognized was that self-imposed or required by the demands of our sport. Unlike the soldier with "Government Issue" stamped on his forehead, we were quite definitely not all cut from one cloth. So it was rather a fit and happy group

The Olympic flame soared from the cauldron into a cloudless sky during the opening ceremony.

131

As host country, the Japanese marched in last in the procession of nations. The U.S. team is closest to the track in Stetsons and blue blazers.

of talented free spirits who more or less assembled to await their turn to march into the stadium. Because the order of the march was alphabetical, we were near the end of the procession of nations, with the Soviets (U.S.S.R.) behind us.

Within the U.S. contingent, the women were in front, with the men lined up behind by height. That put me in the fourth rank behind Conn Findlay and John Thomas, the high jumper, and most of the guys on the basketball team. As with most parades, those at the end of the column wait a long time to get going, and while I was anticipating awe at what I imagined would be a rare moment in my young life, my compatriots were either engaged in outrageous banter with the girls to the front or spirited jive with each other. If the approaching pageantry or anxiety over their competition was troubling them, it did not show. As we shuffled along, starting and stopping, Thomas would wheel on Walt Hazzard (a

basketballer from U.C.L.A.) and say, "Draw." Then in lightning moves each would see who could get his fly down fastest. I'm not sure how they judged the winner, but their irreverence served to send us into the stadium in a happy mood.

As we emerged into the sunlight of the concrete oval filled to its nearly 100,000 capacity, we were deluged with cheers and applause. It cascaded down the rows, washing over us in wave after wave. More than just a moment in sport, it was an international catharsis, a ceremonial coming together in peace and even love of two nations who a brief nineteen years earlier had been locked in mortal combat. Vanquished welcomed victor on equal footing. Welcome was the operative verb. As we marched past the athletes of the other nations standing behind their standard bearers in the infield on our left, and finally the emperor in the royal box on our right, I discovered tears in my eyes and for that moment was 99

Top: Yoshinori Sakai on his way up the stadium steps to light the flame. He was born on the same day the atom bomb was exploded over his home town, Hiroshima. Above: Official Program cover for the Games.

percent proud American and only 1 percent individual oarsman.

Before we had properly taken up our station on the infield, the stadium erupted again with thunderous applause as the Soviets marched in, in step, led by long-time world champion weight lifter, Yuri Vlasov. The Japanese played no politics. They were simply cheering the finest athletes in the world, from rowing's Ivanov to shot-putter Tamara Press. As I watched them pass by, I wondered which ones were in the Soviet eight that had rowed such a brilliant, heartbreaking race in Amsterdam. We had not seen them out at Toda.

When everyone was in place, the emperor welcomed us. Imagine being in a land with a real live emperor! Nineteen years after the surrender, the emperor still ruled due to the foresight and stubbornness of the American Caesar, Douglas MacArthur, as opposed to being executed as were a number of Japanese military leaders.

Then, with little rhetoric, Avery Brundage, president of the International Olympic Committee and passionate (some say fanatic) defender of amateurism, declared the Games open and some white-clad sailors marched in bearing the Olympic flag, which would fly over the stadium throughout the competition.

Yoshinori Sakai, a trim, nineteen-year-old Japanese athlete, the final runner of more than five thousand who carried the torch around the world for these Games, appeared with the Olympic flame held aloft and ran up the steep stadium steps to light the official flame. I wondered if running steps was part of his training program. He did not falter and the cauldron erupted in a blaze of flame. I learned later he was born in Hiroshima on August 6, 1945, the day we dropped the atomic bomb there, and the decision to have him light the flame symbolized Japan's rebirth. He became a world-class runner, although he never competed in the Olympics.

While it was before the days of exploding scoreboards or those with televised images, the one in Tokyo was big and functional and we all looked when the Olympic Creed flashed up in French and English while Mr. Brundage recited it:

The most important thing in the Olympic Games is not to win but to take part, just as the most important thing in life is not the triumph but the struggle.

The Olympic creed by Baron Pierre de Coubertin, founder of the modern Olympics, displayed on the giant scoreboard in the stadium.

It was the first time I'd seen the Olympic Creed or even knew there was one, and my immediate thought was, "Bullshit, I'm here to win." It seemed almost un-American and poles apart from the oft-quoted statement attributed to football coach Vince Lombardi, "Winning isn't everything, it is the only thing."

However analyzed and modified in later years, my philosophical musings were but momentary as 10,000 pigeons held in cages around the track were released simultaneously and I quickly learned another profound truth of international competition: If you are marching in opening ceremonies where they turn pigeons loose, do not look up. I did, of course, and felt my spirit soaring as those birds flew skyward. It was a magical but fleeting moment as we turned and marched out of the stadium into the heart-stopping reality of the regatta.

CHAPTER 12

The Heat

I MAY HAVE SLEPT THAT SATURDAY NIGHT AFTER the opening ceremonies since the heats for the eights were not scheduled until Monday
morning, although the regatta started Sunday for the small boats. After
all the cold rain it was lovely and sunny, and the Toda rowing course had
taken on a festive air when we got out there that Sunday. Flags were flying
everywhere, and the course was lined with flowers installed overnight by
thousands of Japanese workers. Spectators, racing colors, and determination were also much in evidence, making us finally aware that the days
and hours and miles of practice were finished. We put our boat in the
water and took a few strokes, more for something to do than anything
else. Then we took it out and began the effort to focus.

It must have worked as I remember nothing of the endless inter-
vening hours before finding myself in the middle of the race of my life
that Monday morning.

SUNDAY, OCTOBER 11, 1964—My thoughts are funny now at the
eleventh hour—scared, eager, dreading, confident. Not at all what
they should be, I suppose, before an Olympic race. I know it's going
to hurt, and I'm wondering if I got the guts. Don't have the confidence in the boat to row as high as we have to. And yet we've never
rowed a bad race—even on June 6 when I caught a crab it wasn't a
bad race. Maybe the Germans have me cowed, I don't know. Then

in other moods, I'm determined as hell and God and Country and all that stuff. I remember Bill Queen[56] in Metamora as I left after having dinner with him and Betty and Suzy. He was serious just for that moment as he wished me luck and I guess that helps as much as anything else when I think about it. Don't know if I have any inner strength at all or whether I lean on others and draw my strength from them. I guess if you don't have any inner strength you're out of luck in a race cause you're all alone. I just hope we row well enough so I can do a good job and it's not rushed and a lot of work on the recovery. Concentration, that's the thing. If we row that way we'll be right in there. Sometimes I think about sex and a girl I want to sleep with and maybe what I'll do after the competition. My back aches a little now but I don't think it will bother me during the race. Slower than the Germans again today—two 500s at 1:26—Ratzeburg at 1:24, although Dietrich said they had a sheltered lane. God bless Dietrich.

Fourteen nations had entered eights, which meant three heats, two with five boats, one with four. The winners of each of the heats would go directly to the final on Thursday, while all the losers would race in three *repêchage* heats, which would round out the field of six. Of course, we had known for more than a week we would face the Germans in that first heat, and I suppose I had taken a fatalistic view. In retrospect it seemed a little like the Charge of the Light Brigade. I was long past reasoning why. I was going to come home carrying my shield or on it. If we were to lose, as I thought inevitable, it would not be because I had anything left. I had been gathering myself for four years for that moment, and I was determined (an inadequate word) that I would put in the absolute ultimate effort, that I would welcome the pain, that I would not live a lifetime knowing, believing I could have done more. Winning, even losing, at that moment when we backed into the lane

56 A horseman who had fought the Japanese in the Pacific and whose friendship I treasured.

two starting platform was nowhere in my thought.

With Ratzeburg in the race, the other crews were irrelevant, but they were there; the Italians to our starboard in lane one, the Aussies and Yugoslavs in lanes three and four, and finally the Germans, away to our port in lane five. Sunny day, flat water, no wind.

Determination is one thing; concentration is another. Most great athletic endeavors flow from a mind in absolute harmony with the body—not necessarily intellectual effort, but a state of being that allows the body to perform at its peak, to act and react in a harmony of motion and effort and stamina and focus. In recent times that state has been called "being in the zone." It occurs at all levels of competition and, sadly, somewhat at random. It is not a state into which you can necessarily will yourself. In the Olympic Games everyone is in shape, everyone is strong, everyone knows how to row. But it is too simplistic to say, as sportscasters are wont, that the race goes to the athlete who wants it the most. That is part of it, but not all.

Having said all that, the time when the need for concentration, focus, is at an absolute premium, is inevitably the time when the distractions are the greatest. We do not compete in a vacuum; the more important the competition, the more the outside, irrelevant world crowds in.

The mass of spectators, the loud good wishes of friends and teammates on the bank, the band and flags, thoughts of God and country and your iron-willed mother in the stands, all these invade your consciousness and compete for your attention. Even more immediate are the other boats, working their way up the free lane on the bank, warming up, trying their starts in the upper 500 meters of the course. Finally the implacable voice of the starter signals the inevitable with his, *"Encore trois minutes...Encore deux minutes...,"* as he calls you to the starting line.

The minutes on the starting platforms are almost unbearable as you wait for the other boats to back in, the aligner to get bows on line, the starter to raise his flag and begin his countdown across the lanes: *"Etats Unis, prêts?..."* You go through the first ten strokes in your mind for

the thousandth time, knowing how crucial yet fraught with danger they are, longing for the settle so you can kick it down, do what you're good at.

Finally, your body coiled for that first three-quarter stroke, you hear the "P" of the starter's *"Partez"* and your muscles explode as the boats boil off the line to the cacophony of five coxswains urging their crews forward in five distinct languages. Robby reverts to Hungarian—you never understood him anyway—but you know what he wants.

Not much pain in the first 500, and maybe that is the problem. Maybe that's why it takes so long to get your head in the boat, despite your promises to yourself to forget the flag and the folks back home, rather to think and be an eight.

But as you churn by the first 500-meter mark, all that extraneous stuff is gone. You're an eight-oared shell, maybe the fastest eight in the world over 2,000 meters.

Because you believe Ratzeburg is faster than you, you know they will

be ahead but you don't look out, you won't look out. They are way off to port anyway so you can't see their puddles even looking back. Still, Robby doesn't sound like we're out of it. Nothing to do but keep sticking it in, 38–39 strokes a minute, as hard as you can pull, each stroke as if it's your last. There will be nothing left.

The last 100 meters of the first heat showed the Americans (foreground) and the Germans dead even.

By the 1,000, the halfway mark, the pain has begun to seep in and promises to increase with each 10, each 20. Now the rest of the eight has faded and it is just you and your partner, your friend in front of you with whom you've rowed so many miles, dreamed so many dreams. Your friend you've loved, and love, and recently hated, yet you take strength from his puddle, surging now, courage from his broad back. Just the two of you, together, doing what you came for, living the final dream.

Robby calls the last 500 and declares we are even, even with the Germans. That you know to be a blatant lie as you haven't seen or heard them the whole race, never even glimpsed the turbulence from their puddles in your peripheral vision. No matter, you can hate Robby later. He's calling for a ten, but you've been doing tens all the way down. You stop hearing him and are alone, all alone in the universe, you and your pain. Your arms turn to cement, your thighs burn, and your lungs will never again get enough air. Time slows and the finish line, which must have been reached long since, keeps receding. With ten to go, legs and arms disassociate themselves from a now tortured soul, but continue to work on their own without guidance or support, as if the mind gave full measure before the body.[57] There is nothing left.

After a time you realize you are no longer rowing. You know it because you cannot row anymore. Nothing works. You know you have lost. You must have lost. The Germans are faster. But somehow you know you have come closer to touching the face of God than ever before in your short life.

Official times on the finish line scoreboard confirm the Germans' 5:54.02 edges out the Americans at 5:54.30—by just 28/100s of a second.

We did lose, by 28/100ths of a second: the Germans' 5:54.02 to our 5:54.30. So Robby may not have been lying after all. The splits showed us less than a second down with 500 to go, and we made up most of that. For a coxswain to miscall a margin that tight is not a lie; it is not even shading the truth. It is creative belief.

We paddled (the others did anyway) into the slip, and I heard Joe Amlong talking. That threw me (as much as a half-dead person can get) into a rage. How dare he be able to talk? Proof positive he had not put out. I wanted to kill him but couldn't even speak to tell him. As I stared at the dock, it was obvious to me I would need help to get out of the boat and I considered asking Kelly,

EIGHT OARS			
HEATS		2000M	
1 ═GER	5	54	02
2 ═USA	5	54	30
3 ▪ITA	6	02	3
4 ═YUS	6	02	43
5 ▪ AUS	6	06	94
6			

57 I have always been proud of photos I've seen of those last 100 meters showing my oar still bending, my puddle still true.

Above: My father, sister Carolyn, and mother in the stands. Right: On my way to reassure my family that we were still very much in it.

who had a hold of Boyce's rigger and was telling us what a great race we'd rowed. Then I rejected that thought, "Naw...," and rolled out on the dock on my hands and knees. Getting my oar up out of the oarlock seemed another insurmountable problem, but as I pondered it, I realized someone had thoughtfully undone the latch, so I slid the oar backward all the way to the throat and somehow managed to lift it those three inches. I did not participate in putting the boat on its rack in the boathouse, although I shuffled along at the five seat holding on. When we went back out by the dock for a photo by the Japanese (to make sure there would be no ringers in the boat the next day), I realized the Ratzeburg guys were still sitting in their boat. It took them half an hour to move.

I began to feel better. By the time I had showered and was walking up to the stands to explain to my anxious family the meaning of that wonderful new word, "*repêchage*," I could feel the strength beginning to flow back into me. For the first time in ten years of rowing I never looked out. For the first time I had pulled literally as hard as I could on each stroke. The Germans had taken half an hour to lift their boat out of the water. Only 28/100ths of a second and Amlong was talking. For the first time, I knew we could win.

Japanese officials shot team photos to ensure no substitutions would be made in the coming races.

MONDAY, OCTOBER 12, 1964—I didn't think we could win the gold until today. I didn't think it on the way to the start and I didn't think it during the race—maybe that's why we lost. I know I didn't look out (first time in my life), and I didn't believe Robby when he told us we were even with 400 meters to go; I never thought they were as close to us as they were. But now I know they definitely are beatable and we mean to do it. It was the same old thing. One, can I hack it? Two, can we win? Maybe not in that order but…For the first I did okay I figure, but with five strokes to go I didn't have it. My mind didn't go chicken, it wanted to do it, but the body just didn't respond. Maybe we'd have won, if…It was funny, because my mind was okay, at least that wasn't the big trouble, but after the race I couldn't seem to move, contemplated asking for help to get out of the boat and finally rolled onto the dock, didn't think I'd have the strength to lift my oar out of the lock and didn't help at all getting the boat in—then I had to sit down.

But about ten minutes later the strength just seemed to flow back in and I felt fine. Funny. I know I haven't put out that kind of effort since the Penn race on the Schuylkill in '59. But I know I can do it again, and better (strong in the last 20) on Thursday.

So I'm not worried about that angle anymore—the pain—I'll welcome it now and will be able to concentrate on just getting there first. Hell of a thing not to have faith in yourself— that race helped me there—more eager and less scared.

We got away to a decent start, stayed up for twenty-five and rowed in third place to the 1,000, with Italy and Australia dropping back and the Yugoslavs beating the Germans. Yugoslavia faded fast. Our third 500 was slow, but we moved in the two tens Robby called and we were a deck down with 500 to go. Even at 400 and see-saw to the finish to be beaten by .28 seconds—both crews at 5:54. Took the bigwigs 10 minutes to figure out who'd won.[58] If we could have put together a decent last 20, we'd have won—if. I guess I wasn't much help, some of the others had more left than me, I was worried I was weak, but I don't think so. We'll get it all out of everyone on Thursday.

Official times for the eight-oared heats.

The Czechs won their heat, beating Canada by a length in 6:03.88, and the Russians had an easy time with France in 6:06, but slower conditions too. So we go in the *repêchage* tomorrow against Korea and Japan which won't hurt us any—Japan is reasonably fast, about a length and a half behind Canada.

58 There were no finish-line cameras or electronic timers in those days. Rather as many as ten men (suitably attired in blazers) sat in ascending order on a movable stepladder at the finish and punched stopwatches when each boat crossed the line. Small wonder there might be some indecision in a tight race.

THE *REPÊCHAGE*

I don't know what the Germans did that Tuesday, but we raced in the *repê-chage*. We were probably lucky as it gave us something to do, something with which to occupy our minds and essentially get us through one whole interminable day. As the final approached with its inevitable "Partez," the hours and minutes seemed to drag unmercifully and rush at the same time. Why couldn't we just wake up and be on the line instead of having to wait and imagine and row and re-row the race in our heads time after time? Yet, I wasn't ready, it was all rushing too fast. Would I ever be ready?

Our worry with the *repêchage* was neither Japan nor Korea, each of whom had finished last in the other two heats. Rather we agonized over all the things you don't have time to think about when you're in against a fast crew: a broken oar lock, jumping a slide, hitting a buoy, catching a crab—any one of the disasterous flukes that could keep you out of the final.

The Japanese, sensing it was their eight's final moment in the rising sun, had nearly 25,000 spectators lining the bank. Few of them, however, heard the blood-curdling "Bonsai!"[59] with which the Japanese took their first stroke or saw them jump the start. Had it not all been so serious, it would have been funny, and I almost smiled as we got under way and waited for the referee to call a false start. Except he didn't.

I forgot for a moment we were in Japan. The host nation has its prerogatives. So with 20 strokes gone we found ourselves a good half length behind, and the Japanese rowing their normal, brisk 52 strokes a minute. No one panicked, however, as we stuck to our race plan, which was to drop it down to 34 for the middle 1,000, and then, regardless of where anyone was, kick it up at the 1,500 as high as we could to work on our "sprint." The theory, of course, was that we had lost to the Germans in the last 10 strokes. That theory, from my view, was ridiculous. I thought we had sprinted the whole 2,000 meters. Whatever, it was a plan.

In any event, we caught and passed the Japanese in that first 500 and

---

59 That's what it sounded like to us (and U.S. troops in WWII) anyway, but what we probably heard was "bansai" or "ten thousand years to the emperor"—more or less.

In a tight finish, Germany's eight with cox (background) crosses the finish line just ahead of the American shell during their heat on the Toda course Monday. The Germans' time was 5:54.02 and the Americans' 5:54.30. (UPI Photo)

VESPER CLUB TOPPED IN EIGHTS

U.S. Double Sculls Crew Gains Finals

Coverage in *Stars and Stripes*— the U.S. Military Newspaper— October 13, 1964.

took it down on cue to slug it out at the unfamiliar and uncomfortably heavy low stroke in the middle of the course.

Coming up to the stands and the crowd, it must have looked as if the Japanese had a chance for an upset—we only had about a length on them—as we were greeted by a great roar. By that time we had forgotten about the other boats, however, and just wanted to get it over with. So we went on up to 38 or so, moving out to more than a length of open water on the Japanese crew right in front of the stands. It must have looked as if we were pouring it on—at 6:01.47, we beat Japan by almost nine seconds— which is not at all what we intended. I was thinking Germans every stroke. Apparently no offense was taken as the Japanese gave us an Imperial Navy flag flown in a 1904 war as a gesture of goodwill. At least Rosenberg said they did. I never saw it. Maybe it hangs at Vesper somewhere.

The eight oared final started at dusk and
ended in the dark with the Japanese shooting
up flares to light the last 500 meters, and
further confuse an already ravaged mind.

CHAPTER 13

The Final

I DON'T KNOW HOW I PUT IN THE time from the *repêchage* to the day of the final. We must have put our boat in the water on Wednesday, the off day, but I don't remember it. The Village had lost its allure, all the color and fanfare becoming uninteresting. Each of us realized there was nothing now between us and the Germans. I wish I could have lived through it with Boyce, but for that time we had grown apart, each of us retreating into our own small worlds. I'm not sure if I thought about the medal, although the possibility of winning was hanging around the fringes of my consciousness. Mostly, I tried to make myself believe I could, I would, put in another effort like Monday's. It was difficult.

WEDNESDAY, OCTOBER 14, 1964—We had a real good, short (3 x 250) workout today. I feel the boat is ready—it never felt sharper. Then came the waiting and the worrying. Ever since Monday I've fought to keep from thinking about the gold—just about the race— not the gold. But I can't do it and I see myself there in front of the stands with the flag going up. But I've thought a lot about the race too and tried to work myself back into the concentration we had Monday. That was our best race, and I am not sure we can reach that pitch again. I think we'll have to to win.

EXIRA

The Mainichi Daily News

TOKYO   FRIDAY, OCTOBER 16, 1964   © The Mainichi Daily News, 1964

K'CHEV RESIGNS

Kosygin   Khrushchev   Brezhnev

—Kosygin New Premier, Brezhnev 1st Secretary—

MOSCOW, Oct. 15 (UPI)—Premier and Communist Party leader Nikita S. Khrushchev has been retired because of age and his posts taken by two aides, reliable sources said today.

Of course we had not raced the Soviets, but Al told us not to worry about them. I didn't. I knew if we beat Ratzeburg that would be enough. I was reading a book called *The White Nile*, which was intended to keep my mind off sex and help me sleep. It wasn't much good for either. I went to bed that Wednesday night and prayed for sleep.

I awoke at 4 a.m., grateful for six hours. I figured that was enough. I had been worrying about getting to sleep that final night, if it ever happened, for more than a year. I looked out first—every oarsman does—at the flags and the trees to see if there was a wind. No wind. I knew it didn't mean anything nearly twelve hours before race time, but it was comforting nonetheless.

That was the beginning of a long day. The wind kicked up, of course, and by the time the coxed fours went off after lunch it was blowing briskly off the port bow, leaving lanes five and six well sheltered. When a lightly regarded Canadian straight pair (spares for their eight) won the gold in lane six (tragedy for the Dutch, silver, and Germans, bronze), FISA chairman Thomas Keller promptly and properly stopped the racing. We watched it on television back at the Village, delaying our departure for the race course. Naturally we immediately acquired a new set of worries. What if the wind didn't die down or change directions? What if they postponed it until Friday? How could we survive a day without a workout? The thought of trying to get through another night was terrifying. But Keller couldn't do that, could he?[60]

Finally we got the word, so we grabbed our bags, carefully packed hours before with our racing colors, and wended our way through the Village to the bus. There we found the members of the Soviet eight. Who planned that little get-together, I don't know, but they were just about the

60 Years later, Keller would recall the finals in Tokyo were for him a recurring nightmare.

last people with whom I wanted to spend the next hour in close quarters. I expect they felt likewise. That morning, October 15, 1964, the news had reached the Village of the ouster of Nikita Khrushchev, the Soviet Union's premier. All day we had seen the familiar figures in their CCCP sweats grouped around looking at newspapers or wandering about in a daze. Small wonder.[61]

But that wasn't my problem. Having to ride out with the Soviets gave me something else to be mad at our managers about, which was probably as good a mental state to be in as any.

When we got to the course, it was crowded with folks in a holiday mood—and the races had been postponed again. It must have been nearly four o'clock. We repaired to our designated quarters and tried to rest on our tatami mats. All the "what ifs" came crowding back in. There seemed a real possibility we would not race that day.

Then, after another interminable wait, Dietrich banged through the door summoning us with his usual subtlety, "Let's beat those fucking Krauts." With that Germanic exhortation, we peeled off our sweats and headed for the boat. Dietrich, who was and is at his best in regatta logistics, had checked the riggers on our boat about twenty minutes before and found all the nuts loose. Wonder how...? Never mind.

Walking to the boat shed we heard "The Star-Spangled Banner" and applause coming from the finish line. Conn, Ed, and Kent Mitchell had won the gold in the coxed pair. As we took our boat off the rack they carried theirs in, medals around their necks, and wished us luck. Ed did anyway. If ever I wanted to trade places with anyone, it was at that moment. Boyce and I had beaten them, hadn't we? The poignant moment passed, and we were on our way to the start, up past the stands. As we rowed by the winner's dock, the band, and the flags, beginning to work into our warmup, I thought the next time I came by it would all be over. Would I be standing there...? I quickly knocked that off, however, as profitless and

---

61 After the regatta we would smuggle Soviet oarsmen out of the Village in USA sweat suits, thus eluding their Communist keepers there to thwart anyone thinking of defecting.

Conn Findlay, Ed Ferry, and Kent Mitchell on their way to winning the gold in the coxed pair.

told myself to concentrate on the first stroke, keeping it buried, coming out cleanly, getting my hands away quickly for the next crucial half stroke.

It was almost dark. We had lane six, the Germans off to our starboard in lane three.[62] The wind was still blowing but straight up the course, or so they say. Couldn't worry about that, had to remember to keep my hands low on the recovery, the blade high in the choppy water. Didn't want to give the Germans half a second off the start. Wanted it to be clean so we could swing into our settle and start to pound it. It was twilight now, past six o'clock, but I could see Boyce and the starter.

FRIDAY, OCTOBER 16, 1964—It was Conn Findlay's kind of water, choppy and slow. By the time I was down roughing my oar handle[63] and taking my final ablutions Dietrich was moving the buttons out one centimeter for the headwind. Al had given us the word: five and 20,[64] settle to 37, tens at 900 and 1,300 meters and up a stroke with 500 to go—kick it in from 250 and blast for the last 20. And a prayer from Bill Knecht.

The straight four, with Nash and Picard, was winning the bronze behind the Danes and the Brits as we put the boat in. Don't remember what I was thinking as we rowed up by the stands, but

62 Lane 1: Yugoslavia, 2: Soviet Union, 3: Germany, 4: Italy, 5: Czechoslovakia, 6: U.S.A.

63 Using a hacksaw blade so it wouldn't slip in my hands when it got wet.

64 The start: five quick strokes, the first at three-quarters slide, then at half, another at three-quarters, a little more on the fourth, full on the fifth; then 20 high before settling to the racing beat.

it was getting a little dark and the Olympic flame stood out pretty clear—it was now or never. The water was so rough in the first 1,000 meters, especially in our lane, that I was scared to death—envisioning us wallowing down the course slapping waves. I got a resigned sort of "what the hell" feeling and just figured to do the best I could, with a mental note to keep my hands low. Seymour and Jim Storm[65] passed us at the 1,000-meter mark—working hard, almost even with the Russians. Most all the eights were late getting on the line and we got the *"Encore trois minutes,"* before we were half through our warm-up—took only one practice start—that worried me too. So there we were sitting on the start in lane six...

"Encore deux minutes." Christ, it takes forever. Then the long call across the lanes, *"Soviet Union, prêts?...Allemagne, prêts?...Etats-Unis, prêts ?..., Messieurs, êtes-vous prêts?...Partez."* And we were gone.

For some reason or other I was not focused. Sometime in the first 500 it seemed my oar was going through the water awfully easily. I wondered that it didn't hurt more, then consoled myself with the thought that it would hurt soon enough. In fact, we had had a very good start and were handling the rough water well. I was in some sort of never-never-land; rowing, rowing as hard as I knew or could, but with the body somehow disengaged from the brain. The passion, the determination, the concentration that had dominated the first heat had all dissipated. Of course I looked out. I always looked down my blade at the finish anyway, and it took only a fractional shift of the eyes to look a bit farther to starboard. As we were in lane six all the other boats, including the Germans, were to starboard. Trouble was I couldn't see much because it was dark. The Czechs were in lane five next to us in blood-red shirts. Nobody seemed to have much of a lead.

So I rowed along, waiting for the pain and the 1,000-meter mark, both of which arrived about the same time. The Germans were wearing their long-sleeved white jerseys with the black stripe, and that time when

65 U.S. double scull; they would win the silver after leading into the last 500.

I looked over it was pretty clear it was going to be another two-boat race. They had maybe a seat on us. I confess to the shameful and cowardly thought that if it was, indeed, going to be another stroke-for-stroke, win-at-the-wire race like Monday, the silver was nothing to be ashamed of. For one fleeting moment as we passed the 1,000, I doubted I had the courage to repeat Monday's optimum effort.

The moment passed, however, and I took no action on it—continuing to row along as I had been, presumably as hard and well as I could, but with the brain still free-floating outside the body.

Then, in the gloom, the unbelievable began to unfold. At first it was imperceptible. I wasn't sure. I was trying to row, too, after all, and it was dark, but at 1,250 meters it was clear they were a half a length down. The World Champion Ratzeburg eight began to fade. This was certainly something to ponder. We had not been sprinting or taking power tens or anything. Quite incredible really, but nothing to count on. The idea of actually winning was still nowhere near the glimmer of a thought.

Rightly so. For just about then, as I was rowing along thinking how tired I was, my blade slapped a wave on the recovery and spun in my hands so that when I got up to the catch that lovely cupped Karlish blade was backward. I don't know how I knew it was backward, but I did. Never

The final in the dark. The American eight is barely visible in the far lane.

having experienced that precise misadventure before, I did not know precisely what to do. Since we were rowing about 37 strokes a minute, there was not a lot of time for mental debate, but I concluded it would be unwise to put the oar in the water. So I pulled what the Brits called an "air shot," taking the stroke in sync with the others with the blade clear of the water, and frantically twisted the oar handle around properly at the end of the stroke when it was in on my body. On my next trip up the slide, I decided the others could row it in. I was going to make sure I did not mess up, catch a crab, or do something equally catastrophic.

It was so dark I don't think anybody noticed. The boat kept on churning, but Robby said he saw it, and Boyce claims to have started to pray.[66] Life for all of us might have been different after that murky moment of high drama—one of those things that can make your palms sweat, even fifty years later.

From then on my blade was eighteen inches off the water on each recovery, while my hands bumped along the top of my legs. I did not hit any more water. I kept on rowing in the same sort of disembodied way and kept on watching the Germans who now seemed nearly a length behind. I couldn't see anybody else. It was too dark.

With 500 to go, I was very much worried about a German sprint and not feeling much like sprinting myself. Then there was a bright explosion and another, and I had something else for my ravaged brain to focus on. Could we have passed the finish line? Had I so miscalculated? But they don't shoot off guns at the Olympic finish, and, spaced out though I was, I knew we had only rowed 1,500 meters. Robby was saying something but he had lapsed into Hungarian again, and I couldn't hear him anyway because of the now intermittent explosions.

In any case, it seemed prudent to keep on rowing, so I did, and kept on watching Ratzeburg, who didn't seem to be coming. I say "seem" a lot because it was all becoming surreal. The sky had brightened in a patchy

66 In later years my friend Budd has derived considerable pleasure in pointing out I took one stroke less than the rest of the crew.

Waiting in the dark for the Germans after getting our medals: we pulled the boats together while they gave us their shirts.

sort of Fourth-of-July way, and there was considerable noise from the stands even though we were way across in the far lane. Crowd noise is always good in a boat race because, ahead or behind, it means you are going to get to stop rowing soon. But while I felt it very worthwhile to keep an eye on those white shirts with the black stripe, I was still not thinking about winning.

A medal, any medal, was a long way from my mind. Rather I was still very concerned about the possibility of having to sprint. I thought I could sustain the groove of pain I was in, but was not sure I could crank it up to a more exquisite level. Long before it was proper, I began longing for the finish. Robby should at least have been saying, "thirty more," or something. Maybe he was blinded by the explosions. It turned out the Japanese were shooting up flares to light the finish. They thought of everything.[67] But I was still cussing Robby silently as he refused to tell us where the damned finish line was.

67 Actually, Thomas Keller thought of them. In a 1979 interview in *The Oarsman* he recalled, "The final of the eights had to be started when it was already dark. Having considered this possibility in advance, we had previously asked the Japanese Army to provide vehicles and flares just in case we might need them. In an incredibly dramatic race the Americans managed to beat the Germans on a course which for the last 500 meters was illuminated by flares. These, however, proved to be different from the ones I know from our Army as they kept on burning all the way down until they fell into the water. When I realized this all I could do was to pray that none of them would land on an oarsman's back. Thank heavens we were lucky."

Then, by some intuitive impulse, we stopped rowing. As the Germans put in another four or five strokes, it seemed as though we had won. But it didn't matter. All the baloney about winning and losing could wait. I was grateful just not to be rowing anymore.

We sat there for a while in the dark. With the race over the flares had all faded, nobody was saying much, no whooping and hollering—just quiet, away from everybody in that outside lane, slumped over our oars. Boyce may have reached back and grabbed my ankle. He usually did when we won and was too tired to either turn around or talk. That large, firm grip said whatever was worth saying.

Then Robby started hollering at us, telling us we had to row over to the stands. When we got to the winners' dock, everybody else was hollering at us, which was nice, but loud, and somehow kind of irrelevant. It turned out our 6:18.23 put us some five seconds ahead of the Germans—6:23.29—with the Czechs third. I was not anywhere near as gone as after that first heat, but mentally, emotionally I was out of it, exhausted. Thirteen months of striving, fear, anticipation, and determination were over, dissipated in a little over six minutes. The focus of my life had evaporated, and I was coming out of a long dream into a new, strange world.

I didn't know all that, of course. I just knew I was very tired, and as we struggled out of the boat and arranged ourselves to face the floodlights

Watching the flag raising as the Japanese band played the "Star Spangled Banner."

Vesper Upsets Germans by 1¼ Lengths for Rowing Title

U.S. SHELL AHEAD AFTER 800 METERS

Philadelphia Eight Topples Defender—American Pair With Coxswain Is First

By JAMES ROACH
Special to The New York Times

TOKYO, Oct. 15—When the band played "The Star-Spangled Banner" after the seventh and last championship race of the Olympic rowing program today, there were, most appropriately, bombs bursting in air.

That last event of a wind-delayed show was held half an hour after sundown. And with settling over the Toda flares

HAPPY WINNER: Lesley Bush after winning gold medal in platform diving.

had won eight straight Olympic titles between 1920 and 1956. Then, in 1960 at Rome, the Ratzeburg Rowing Club of Hamburg won for Germany. To Ratzeburg, which had beaten a preliminary

via fourth, the highly regarded Soviet Union boat fifth and Italy last. Vesper's time was 6 minutes 18.23 seconds.

Young Jack Kelly, the great sculler whose father won three Olympic sculling titles in 1920 and 1924, said jubilantly at the boat house, "This puts America right back on top in rowing."

As Vesper's secretary-treasurer, the brother of Princess Grace of Monaco is credited with starting to plan for today's triumph as soon as he returned from Rome in 1960.

Vesper is an unusual crew. Only three men—the No. 3, Emory Clark; the No. 6, Boyce Budd, and the stroke, Bill Stowe—rowed in college. Clark and Budd are Yale men. Stowe, a Navy lieutenant senior grade, went to Cornell.

The others are First Lieut. Joe Amlong of the United States Air Force, the bow; Hugh Foley, a student at La Salle College, No. 2; Stan Cwiklinski, another La Salle student, No. 3; First Lieut. Tom Amlong, No. 4, and Bill Knecht, Joe's

Medal Winners

	Gold (18)	Silver (20)	Bronze (20)
United States	15	7	10
Soviet Union	8	4	6
Japan	7	2	3
Germany	3	6	4
Australia	2	1	1
Bulgaria	2	1	0
Hungary	2	0	1
Britain	1	1	1
Poland	1	1	1
Turkey	1	0	0
Netherlands	0	2	2
Czechoslovakia	0	2	0
Canada	0	1	1
Denmark	0	1	0
Finland	0	1	0
Rumania	0	1	2
France	0	0	2
Italy	0	0	2
Cuba	0	1	0
Korea	0	1	0
Tunisia	0	0	1
Iran	0	0	1
Sweden	0	0	1
Switzerland	0	0	1

fected from the Hungarian crew in Melbourne in 1956.

The coach is Al Rosenberg, for 10 years a Vesper coxswain. He's an attorney on leave from the City Attorney's Office in Philadelphia.

Vesper rowed in a 57-foot Italian-made shell and used 12-foot-5-inch German oars in the wide-scoop ends. Cost of the medal-winning boat and oars.

bow: Dr. Charles W. Riggall Jr., a dentist, is Vesper's president.

Nelson F. Cox, the Princeton boatman, spent the early hours of the afternoon polishing the boat, sandpapering one spot, oiling seat-slides, washing the boat with soap compound, washing it with clear water and drying it with the care a mother gives a brand-new offspring.

The Soviet Union's great single sculler, Vyacheslav Ivanov, who has the title Merited Master of Sports of the U.S.S.R., won his third straight Olympic title in his specialty. Last Sunday, Don Spero, a Columbia graduate student, beat Ivanov in a heat. This time, Spero was last.

The gold medalists included the American pair with coxswain. At the oars were F. Conn Findlay of Belmont, Calif., the nonpaid rowing coach at Stanford, and Ed Ferry of Seattle, a Navy ensign who rowed with Findlay in his days at Stanford.

The coxswain, riding up forward stretched out on his back and enjoying Olympic life to the utmost, was Kent Mitchell, a brand-new 115-pound member of the California bar. The upfront, stretched-out position wind resistance.

Red Smith
Vesper Had a Plan and It Worked

TOKYO, Oct. 15

THE American crew, said the lady announcer on the public address system, would now receive gold medals from "Mistah Blundage." It had been a long, hard day for Slavery Avery Brundage, chief medal-hanger at Tokyo's monster muscle dance.

All afternoon he'd been dishing out hardware for first, second and third places in the Olympic rowing finals, festooning winners was easy for a stand-up guy like Avery, because winners get out of their boats and take their trophies standing at attention while the band plays their national anthem and their country's flag creeps up the tallest flagpole.

Crews finishing second and third, though, take their silver and bronze medals sitting down in their shells. For them, the unbending president of the International Olympic Committee had to bend. Every time he stooped, his shirt cracked.

Even so, this may have been Avery's finest hour. For here he was, an American under a big, silver Japanese moon hanging gewgaws on eight Americans and an expatriate Hungarian who had restored boatracing supremacy to the United States by rowing through the Japanese dark with German oars in an Italian shell to win the classic eight-oared event and keep the faith with an Irish-American sponsor whose bricklayer father disliked the British. "And the rockets' red glare," the band played, "the bombs bursting in air." And as though on cue, rockets glared, bombs burst.

It had been a gloriously bright day with a temperature of 71, but a bad day for rowing because of the wind. It blew about 16 miles an hour and it kept shifting direction but it was always against the oarsmen and mostly it came from off the port bow, making hideously unfair conditions.

The lane on the far left, No. 6, was in the lee of a steep bank. In the day's first race the boats finished 6-5-4-3-2-1, exactly in order of their position off that lee bank.

The Toda rowing course, 45 minutes by kamikaze taxi from downtown Tokyo, is a perfectly straight canal dug especially for the Olympics and otherwise useless.

* * *

THE first race, four oars with coxswain, was won by Germany and when it ended the cox stood up like a landlubber and clambered forward to smooch each of his shipmates. Kissed, the bow oar swooned, lying flat on his back on the forward deck. For a while it looked as though the crowd would see a burial at sea.

Yankees qualified for five of the seven finals and they did wonderfully well, taking two gold medals, one silver and one bronze. They began, however, with a painful disappointment when Don Spero, an escapee from Cornell working for his doctorate at Columbia, finished sixth and last in the single sculls. Spero had hoped to win, for in his qualifying heat he had made Russia's merited master of sports, Vyacheslav Ivanov, quit cold.

Ivanov, Olympic winner in 1956 and 1960, had been practically unbeatable for 10 years and Spero has been sculling only a year and a half. After clobbering the commie in their heat, however, Spero came up with a bad back and Ivanov creamed all the others for his third straight title.

The wild and erratic wind had everybody in a sweat. The first race was delayed an hour and a half in the vain hope that the breeze would abate. As waves kicked up in the watery ditch it was announced that the single sculls had been postponed, but the next thing spectators knew, the scullers were racing. Pair oars with coxswain followed, and America's huge team won that with a smashing sprint which so cooked the Russian pace-setters that they finished fourth.

We got a third in the four oars without cox, a second in the double sculls, and then here came the eights, the main event. This is a race that America won eight times in a row from 1920 through 1956 before the unbeatable

Ratzeburg crew, of Germany, murdered everybody in 1960.

After those games in Rome, young Jack Kelly went home to Philadelphia and set about building a crew at the Vesper Boat Club to win the 1964 Olympic. Young Jack's father, who was also the sire of Princess Grace of Monaco, won the single sculls in 1920 and took the doubles with Paul Costello in 1920 and 1924. He got sore at the King of England because he wasn't allowed to go for the Diamond Sculls at Henley, limited in those days to gentlemen who had never worked with their hands, and Jack Kelly had laid brick.

* * *

JACK trained up a son who did not work with his hands, did win the Diamond Sculls, but went through four Olympics without getting a title. That's why young Jack spent his own money to build this Vesper crew and keep it going. Only three of the eight had done any serious rowing in college. The cox, Bob Zimonyi, steered three Olympic crews for Hungary and defected after the 1956 games in Australia.

Sixty years had passed since a club crew last represented the United States in the eight-oared race. Vesper rowed in 1900 and 1904 and won both times, so Vesper is undefeated in the Olympics. This year the college crews, who wanted no truck with gents' rowing clubs, tried to keep Vesper out of the American tryouts but Kelly threatened to go to court and the committee backed down. Vesper thereupon won the trials.

Now this motley mob set off down the Toda canal, and night had fallen. Flares burned on both banks of the course to mark the finish line. The Japanese, who love fireworks, kept shooting off rockets that burst into flares hung on tiny parachutes. The great German crew led for 690 of the 2000 meters, but the Americans had a plan.

Allen Rosenberg, the tiny lawyer-pharmacist who coaches Vesper, had told 'em to spurt at 800 meters, at 1200 and at 1400, figuring that one spurt had to take them to the front. They got a lead at 800, increased it at 1200 and blew the race apart at 1400. At the 2000-meter finish, approximately a mile and a quarter, they had a length and a quarter on the Germans. They didn't pitch coxswain Zimonyi into the drink, as tradition demands. "Tomorrow," he pleaded when they laid hands on him. "Tonight I could get a heart attack."

my mind was empty. That worried me. I thought of my family, proud up there somewhere behind the lights. I thought that this moment, with Avery Brundage about to put a gold medal around my neck, should be one of the profound moments in my life. I wondered why I was not thinking profound thoughts, something I could tell my grandchildren. But I wasn't. I was just profoundly happy to be breathing, huge, sweet lungfuls of air. I reveled in that simple pleasure as the Stars and Stripes went up and the Japanese Marine Band played "The Star-Spangled Banner."

FRIDAY, OCTOBER 16, 1964—The presentation ceremony was fantastic with the Olympic flame and the flares, and the darkness, and the lights in our eyes. I wasn't as tired as Monday, but it just seemed easier to crawl out of the boat, so I did. Somebody helped me up and we stood there—Mr. Brundage put gold medals around our necks—I forgot to stoop—and Mr. Keller shook our hands. Then the flag and the Star-Spangled Banner—I had thought I would cry at that time if it ever came, but I was too tired and just stood there and watched it and enjoyed being able to breathe—deep sweet breaths that just felt so good.

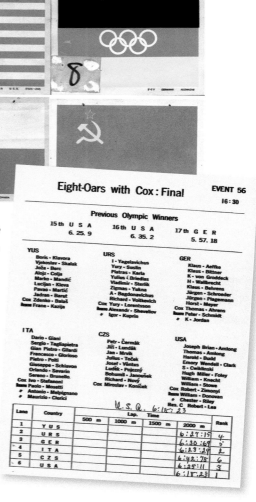

Above: Boat rack markers from the Toda boat house— USA, Germany, Czechoslovakia, and the Soviet Union. *Below:* Finals times for the Eights in my mother's handwriting.

Farewell to the Flame

IT WASN'T A RACE TO BE PROUD OF; it was a race to be thankful for. Unlike Monday, there was no ultimate anything. But there was winning. Winning makes up for a lot of less than perfection. I learned then you never give the medal back.

The Germans were first-class sports. In fifty years I've never heard an excuse. Possibly we had a sheltered lane, although I've been told the wind was dead on head. Certainly it was a lot longer race than the heat, 29 seconds for the Germans, 24 for us. An eternity in any last 500. Nor did we suddenly sprint. Each crew rowed each 500 meters slower than it had rowed the previous one. Ratzeburg was leading at the 1,000 by a fraction of a second, as I suspected. They simply slowed down in the third 500 more than we did. Five seconds. Open water. Unbelievable, really.

We waited up the course a bit while the Germans collected their medals, then pulled the boats together there in the dark. They gave us their shirts and shook hands. Nothing much to say. I still have that shirt.[68]

Years later, in 1978, after the World Championships at Lake Karapiro

---

[68] I don't know why we didn't give them our shirts; didn't think about it, I suppose. But I know we didn't as I wore mine years later while while running the Olympic flame before the 1996 Atlanta Games.

Boat club pride

in New Zealand, I found myself getting reasonably smashed in the company of Jürgen Plagemann, Ratzeburg's two man in Tokyo. After considerable inner debate, I summoned the courage to ask him what was still to me a delicate question: "What happened to you, why did you lose it in the third 500?" Jürgen, then director of the Ruderakademie Ratzeburg, and against whom I have since rowed several times in veterans' regattas, took so long to answer I thought he was offended. Finally he said simply, "We rowed too hard to the 1,000."

I am certain we won the gold in the first heat. That was the race that convinced us we could win, and, I think, convinced the Germans they could be beaten. They were all Olympic and World Champions. To win in the Games you have to have it on the day. If there is a headwind and choppy water, well, you have to cope with it.

In Munich in '81 while discussing the matter with Ratzeburg's six man and three-time Olympian Karl-Heinrich von Groddeck (again after a great deal of beer), I was going to conclude by suggesting we were evenly matched and that if we had raced five times Ratzeburg might have won three, Vesper two, or vice versa. Karl would have none of it, however, quickly interrupting with, "We'd have won four," before I could finish my thought. Fair enough.

None of that mattered to us back then in the dark Japanese night as we paddled slowly back to the boat sheds to be swallowed up in an enthusiastic sea of well-wishers. I think it was at that moment we ceased being a crew. One of my first thoughts, standing on the dock, tired and wet, was that I didn't care if I ever saw the Amlongs again—a thought much more unkind in the telling than it probably was. Just as my mind was blank, so my emotions were empty. My feelings toward Tom and Joe were really non-feelings. They were part of the pressure I was shedding. I did not

The morning after—A command performance after a night without sleep.

have to care about them anymore. My feeling then toward Boyce may have been much the same, but I knew when feeling returned I would love him again. Perhaps there was an unconscious sadness, an emptiness at the as yet unarticulated awareness that the '64 Vesper eight was no more.

It was there on the slip Bill Knecht and I made a pact that we would sign our Christmas cards, "From one Gold to Another"—and we did that every year until Bill died in 1992.

I hugged my sister, Carolyn, loving her and worrying that I was getting her wet. I don't remember seeing my brother, Bill, but I knew he had been in the stands, which mattered enormously. He had seen me quit against Harvard four years before, and knew what he was watching. Now, perhaps, I had come partway back. My mother, I knew, would be fiercely proud, although not surprised, while my father would be the toast of the town back in Detroit. I began to realize something very good had happened when I saw Boyce's father. He appeared to be the happiest man in Tokyo.

The regatta party that night was typical, but I was still out of it, not inclined to drink much. I didn't need to really. I knew the gold medal would be there to savor, that I would wake up to greet it in the morning, and all the mornings after that. The Aussies, always winners at the party, did their usual thing without pants, hanging from the chandelier, or maybe

VERY VERY PROUD TO KNOW YOU

HIG

CQLLN OB140 W U.S.

CONGRATULATIONS WE KNEW YOU WOULD BRING BACK THE GOAL IF

YOU HAVE OPPORTUNITY STOP IN SEATTLE AS EVER YOUR OLD

COACH

RON

OCT 17 0822

BEAUTIFUL JOB EM CONGRATULATIONS TO EVERYONE

ENJOY YOURSELF DOWN UNDER

TOM

CONGRATULATIONS FROM THE BARRONS

ALL BARRON

DETROIT SHARES THE PRIDE OF METAMORA IN YOUR ROWING EXPLOITS

AT THE OLYMPIC GAMES THE PERFORMANCES OF THE UNITED STATES

TEAM PRODUCED MANY THRILLS TO THE PEOPLE AT HOME AND HIGH

ON THAT LIST WAS THE WINNING EIGHT IN ROWING

JEROME P CAVANAGH MAYOR CITY OF DETROIT

OCT 23 0

Telegrams
from home

EMORY CLARK US OLYMPIC ROWING TEAM TOKYO

GOOD GUYS FINISH FIRST HAPPINESS YOURE WRONG

SUSAN

CONGRATULATIONS ON TERRIFIC JOB

WHEN ARE YOU COMING HERE

OSTHEIMER

OCT 16 2

ELATED BY VICTORY

DIANE AND HERRICK

COLL OD054

HUZZAH IN YOUR FINEST GRANDSTAND TRAIDITION YOU FRIGGIN

SHOW OFFS

HOWIE AND MARY

CONGRATULATIONS TO YOU AND THE VESPER CREW,

WINNERS OF THE FIRST OLYMPIC NIGHT RACES WE ARE PROUD

MARYON AND UNCLE LEE

BANZAI

BOBSIE

MAY HEALTH STRENGTH SPEED BE YOURS ALL EIGHT OF YOU

SUZI BROWN

COLL OB047

on a table in the center of the dance floor. There must have been women, but I don't remember any. The huge young bowman from the Soviet coxed pair gave me an exquisitely decorated lacquered spoon, which I have still. I suspect he got it as a gift from a Japanese schoolboy. He was drunk but remembered me from Amsterdam, and was still suffering from the Findlay treatment in the last 500 earlier that afternoon.

After dinner on the town with some of the crew, I split off from the revelers and went back to the Village, not to sleep, just to be. For me, anyway, I do better at reveling when I lose. I wanted to feel it by myself, away from the distraction of my happy teammates. Maybe I sensed the emotional abyss at the edge of which I was standing.

THE LAURELS

The rest of the Games were pure sugar candy. We strutted about with ten more days of free room and board in the Village, while going to all of the events we could get tickets to: soccer, boxing, gymnastics, track, volleyball.

OCTOBER 21, 1964—Spent all morning watching the women's gymnastics—with the Czechs clearly the best—as graceful an outfit as I've ever seen. Ma and Pa and Carolyn and Toca[69] came in the Village for lunch and wandered around some.

Went to boxing again with Ma and Pa—saw Joe Frazier knock out the Russian in a great heavyweight fight. The Russians threw in the towel (literally) in the second round. Seven Russians in the boxing final.

Al, Boyce, Tony J., Chester, Bill Stowe and I went to eat, first at a steak house where they cook it on the table, then at a curry house cause we weren't quite full, and, finally, for dessert at another place—great.

We watched a lot more on the television in our barracks in the Village.

69 A young Japanese woman who was guiding my parents.

Edith McGuire won the 200-meter dash and was second in the 100, and I remember being in the common room with fifteen or twenty other athletes while she was running the last leg of the 4x100 meter relay. We were all intensely interested as each gold medal drama unfolded, so you could have heard a pin drop as Edith took the baton on her leg well behind the woman in the lead. She shot away like a scared jackrabbit, and soon her long, graceful, fluid stride was eating up the distance between her and the leader. As we held our collective breath and it began to look as if she might do it, a deep, awed voice rumbled out of one of the black basketball players, "Look at that nigger run!" That broke us up as we cheered and hollered for Edith, who led her country to a silver medal finish.

After our final, I remember doing two other things as a crew. We went back out to a strangely deserted Toda Rowing Course the next day (seemingly lifeless without flags or flowers), posing for pictures in our racing colors and rowing 30-stroke pieces for an army of Japanese with movie cameras. The Japanese were making a study of each Olympic sport and wanted footage for instructional purposes. I suspect we performed with ill grace as many of us had not been to sleep at all, and those short pieces seemed incredibly exhausting.

Yet another photo op at the behest of the Japanese. From left: J. Amlong, Foley, Cwiklinski, T. Amlong, Zimonyi, Clark, Budd, Knecht, Stowe.

Life magazine's night on the town:
Unwinding at a geisha house after lots
of sake; cavorting nude in a traditional
Japanese bath (girls not shown.)

Then *Life* magazine took us on a tour of Tokyo nightlife that started in a massage parlor and ended hours later at a geisha house. As each of us envisioned his handsome features on the cover, we postured and posed in sophomoric manner throughout the evening until the beer and saki rendered us beyond caring. I had been in Oriental baths before, but none like this one, which was huge, with as many as fifty massage tables in one room. We were each assigned a girl who stripped us nude, then stretched us, kneaded us, steamed us, washed us, and finally placed us in a steaming communal tub while she stood with the other girls and tittered. We naturally assumed, given the human bodies they normally had to deal with, that we gave them plenty to titter about. In any case, when the magazine came out, Don Schollander, handsome, blond, Yale swimmer, was on the cover, while the Vesper eight was buried inside, in the tub, with none of the girls and no muscle worth mentioning in sight. Very disappointing.

The evening itself was not, however. By the time we got to the geisha house we were beginning to like each other again and relaxed under the gentle ministrations of the geishas, just as we were supposed to, while Dietrich made a toast and we modestly acknowledged each other as champions. The Amlongs, of course, still claimed the credit. After that evening we each went our separate ways, and it would be years before we were together again.

One of my separate ways had to do with a tall, slim "hostess" at a Tokyo nightclub called the Queen Bee. She had been much on my mind as I had been trying to banish all thoughts of sex in the days leading up to the regatta. Two years before while down from Mount Fuji on liberty I had made her acquaintance, and, if the truth be known, she was one of the social highlights of my Marine Corps year in the Far East. Would she still be there? Would she remember me? Would I recognize her? Those questions only added pique to my quest, which began after a rather formal dinner with my parents and some proper Japanese friends of theirs to which I had come attired in my Olympic blazer with the medal in my pocket. If I wasn't the prime attraction, the medal certainly was.

A kamikaze cab got me to the Queen Bee where I ventured up to the balcony (the girls who spoke foreign languages were ensconced there), ordered an Asahi beer, and asked after Yoko. She looked quite a bit more than two years older actually, despite her floor-length brocade silk gown, but if she did not recognize me she hid it well. I was certainly a Yank, and she had seen one or two of them in her time.

She took me to a small, clean $3-a-night hotel where Papa San served green tea on our arrival and fussed about considerably before sliding shut the bamboo door to our room. I hung my blazer, together with the medal, on a peg and wondered briefly what the American people would think if they could see this particular flower of American youth at this particular moment. After Yoko and I renewed our acquaintance very satisfactorily in the time-honored fashion, she thought to inquire what brought me back to town, this while we were resting and sipping tea. Her English consisted of ten or twenty words at best, but apparently enough to land her on the balcony. She spoke a certain intimate international language fluently.

While the Japanese as a nation were enthralled with the Olympics, I suspect the Games had had little impact among the ladies of the Queen Bee. Nonetheless, when I pointed to my blazer and told her why I had returned, Yoko gave some evidence of knowing whereof I spoke. Indeed, she put down her tea cup and asked the next question, which prompted me to fish the medal out of the pocket and hand it to her.

At that moment I achieved a social status that no yen could buy, and so did Yoko. In fact, she gathered her kimono about her naked form and rushed out of the tiny, bedless room, causing me acute anxiety as I pondered how I would explain the loss of my gold medal on my return home. Then I heard banging on the sliding doors up and down the corridor, and soon all the other hostesses in varying stages of undress who happened to be stopping at that particular hotel that evening were out in the hall exclaiming in rapidfire Japanese. After examining the medal (the likes of which they had no doubt seen daily on television), there was no way not to examine the owner of same, which they did with considerable enthusiasm. I confess to feeling more than a little ridiculous in the kimono thoughtfully supplied by Papa San, a garment that came to a point only slightly below my hip bones. More exclaiming, and this time I was quite sure I knew what they were talking about.

With all that excitement, Yoko was happy to accommodate me again, after which I slept soundly, perhaps for the first time since the final, until daylight. Dressed, I made my way out onto a wet, deserted street with no idea where I or the Olympic Village was. I don't know how I got back, but when I did the medal was safely in my pocket.

THE GAMES

From my point of view, as well as that of the Japanese, the Games of the XVIII Olympiad were a grand success. And through the prism of history, they may have been regarded as one of the more successful

The 1964 Olympics had more than their fair share of dramatic events and amazing athletes. Gold medalists—from upper left: Bob Hayes, USA, 100 Meter Dash; Abebe Bikila, Ethiopia, Marathon; Iolanda Balas, Romania, High Jump; Billy Mills, USA, 10,000 Meters; Vyacheslav Ivanov, Soviet Union, Single Scull; Vera Caslavaska, Czechoslovakia, Gymnastics

Games in that there was no violence, no boycotts (all the world's best were there), no drugs (or drug testing as far as I know), no terrorism, no political posturing.[70] All the athletes were more-or-less amateurs (although perhaps not by Mr. Brundage's pristine standard), and no one used his or her athletic ability to launch a mega-buck career, either through endorsements or television.[71]

Television, of course, had discovered the Games, but more in a reporting mode and less in the all-pervasive, intrusive, extravagant way the Games are covered today. The coverage was in black-and-white in real time, and the folks back home had to stay up till the wee small hours to see the various events in which they had an interest. Vesper fans not only had to stay up late but didn't get to see much of our final as the course was so dark and we were in the farthest lane from the cameras. None of that impinged on my consciousness at the time, however. Only when I got home nine months later did I learn of the frustration of some of our supporters.

The big news of our day, October 15, was Marine lieutenant and Blackfoot Indian Billy Mills winning the 10,000. Beating the great Australian distance runner, Ron Clarke, his was an upset of at least the same magnitude as ours, and because it came much earlier in the day was in time to make the headlines back home—a fact, again, I only learned much later and which bothered me not at all. He deserved his press.[72] We had our medals.

The Americans, led by future U.S. senator Bill Bradley and Walter Hazzard, won in basketball, beating Brazil.

70 I should say more properly I was blissfully unaware of any political statements being made. I did not know, for instance, that when the South African Olympic Committee refused to denounce apartheid in sports, the IOC, led by American Avery Brundage, revoked South Africa's invitation to Tokyo. I am not sure what I would have thought had I known. Probably not much. South Africa was a long way off, and as far as I knew, did not have any fast eights.

71 In the run-up to the 2012 London Games I agreed to speak at a local elementary school and was asked how much I charged. That surprised me.

72 Years later, a movie was made of Mills's improbable story, *Running Brave*, which met with considerable critical acclaim. At least two movie producers have had a run at making a rowing *Chariots of Fire* out of our Vesper saga but could not find the necessary money or interest in Hollywood. I had fun consulting on scripts and worrying about who would play me, but it never got past the fun stage.

Top left: Pocket patch provided by Kelly when we got home. Bottom left: Pocket from Olympic blazer. Top and bottom right: USA and German racing shirt patches.

Vera Caslavska, the fabulous Czechoslovakian gymnast whom I was lucky enough to see (and fall in love with) won most of the medals in her sport. I fell in love frequently and generally felt as charitable toward my fellow man during those few days as I have at any time in my life.

Bob Hayes, the world's fastest human (and later a Dallas Cowboy), won the 100-meter dash, equaling the world record, and another American, Bob Schul, won the 5,000, giving the United States some success for the first time in the distance events.

Billy Mills ran the marathon, too, but it was won for the second time

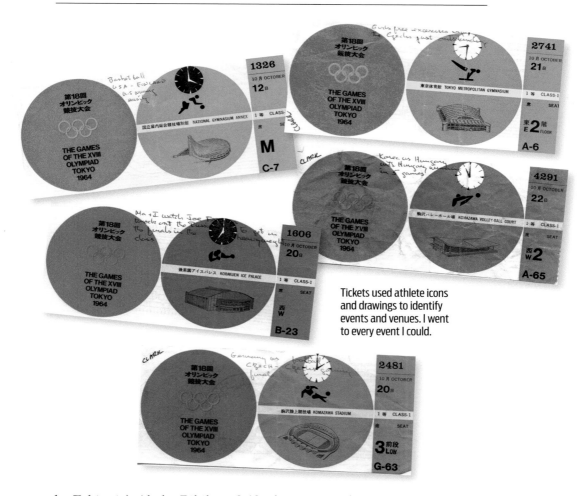

Tickets used athlete icons
and drawings to identify
events and venues. I went
to every event I could.

by Ethiopia's Abebe Bikila in 2:12, this time in shoes. In Rome, he had
run barefoot.

John Thomas, favored to win the high jump, tied with the Soviet,
Valery Brumel, both jumping 7' 1¾", but came away with the silver
because of the number of tries taken to clear the bar.

The mammoth Soviet woman, Tamara Press, won two golds with
the shot put and the discus while her sister, Irena, won the woman's
pentathlon. (Tamara competed before the days of sex tests, and some
doubt was raised as to what one might have revealed. I never saw her in

the shower, but she could certainly put the shot—and looked like a woman to me.) An English woman, Ann Rand, who came second to Irena, was another with whom I fell in love. She was married to a British oarsman and used to ride out to Toda with us on the bus.

In rowing, only three of the seven American crews were out of the medals. The two golds came in the eight and the coxed pair, while Seymour Cromwell[73] and Jim Storm settled for silver in the double after appearing to have the race locked up with 500 to go.

Teddy Nash's straight four won the bronze, losing out for the silver by a fraction of a second to the Brits. By that time we were calling it Picard's four, as Geoff was filling in for an ill Phil Durbrow and did not appear to slow the boat down. We had considerable fun warning Geoff, the only Harvard oarsman friendly with the Vesper contingent, that he better not be seen fraternizing with us or Harry Parker[74] would not let him back in the Harvard eight the following spring.

Don Spero, our single sculler who did well in the heats, faded to sixth in the final, I think with some back trouble. The Russian, Ivanov, won in the single handily, collecting his third gold in three Olympics. Ivanov was a stud.

The Harvard coxed four, coached by Parker in Tokyo, did not make the final, nor did Tony Johnson and Jim Edmunds in the straight pair. Tony and Jim's contribution to our eight by beating the Amlongs back in June has already been gratefully acknowledged. Without that defeat Tom and Joe might never have rowed in the eight.

Since 1964, Olympic gold medals for heavyweight oarsmen have been hard to come by. Lewis and Enquist won in the double in 1984, but the men's eight would not win again for forty years, until 2004, in Athens.

In October of 1964, the sweep of history meant little to me, however. I was living in the present and enjoying it hugely.

73 Seymour had been a senior at Groton School and a prefect in my dorm my first year.
74 Harry Parker coached at Harvard for fifty-one years until his death in June 2013 after one final victory over Yale. His record in the Harvard-Yale race (44-7) is one that Old Blues try their best to forget.

OCTOBER 24, 1964—Found out Frazier won last night with a dislocated finger on his right hand. He'd gotten it fighting the Russian and hadn't told anybody. I wondered why he didn't kill the guy. Just like John Thomas who jumped with a hernia he was determined not to tell anyone about (someone sent him a telegraph saying, "You're a bum."), or Al Oerter with muscles torn off his rib cage when he set the world record with the discus.

Closing ceremony made me cry just like the opening—this time it was just one big long column of athletes all mixed—marched with Picard and an Irish girl—lights out—flame out—flag down—Sayonara on the scoreboard—little girls with torches—waving and clapping and clapping, sounding like rain on the roof. Sayonara party afterwards—Sushi and beer and Japanese dancers and lanterns and *takusanno*[75] autographs.

THE CLOSING

Some of the athletes went home before the closing ceremonies. Some from the Communist countries weren't permitted to stay. But I, in no hurry and possessed of a round-the-world ticket, wanted to savor the Games until the finish line. Like Cinderella, I didn't want the ball to end, and I suspected, rightly, that I would never be privileged to participate in such wonderful doings again.

Unlike the opening ceremonies when we marched into the stadium by country, pride of nation was appropriately set aside for the closing (except properly for the Japanese team). I strolled onto the oval track once again to the cheers and clapping of 80,000 fans, hand in hand with an Irish girl and my new Harvard friend, Geoff Picard. We were a relaxed and happy group of young people who thronged the infield as darkness fell, and we applauded, in turn, the fans who so appreciated us.

For the athletes ceremony was now irrelevant, but we stood patiently through the closing speeches, tolerating the bigwigs, good-naturedly

75 Many.

The closing ceremony summoned up a wellspring of emotion. We were young, passionate and represented the finest athletes in the world.

Athletes of all nations mingle as they march out of Tokyo's National Stadium following the ceremonies that closed the 18th Olympic Games. The informal march-out Saturday night was in sharp contrast to the precision of the opening ceremonies two weeks ago. The scoreboard in the background reads, "We meet again in Mexico City, 1968." The Mexican capital has been selected as the next site of the international spectacular. (S&S Photo by Fred G. Braitsch Jr.)

LAUGHS, TEARS, 'SAYONARA'

clapping at the appropriate times. We watched with a growing sense of sadness and incipient nostalgia as hundreds of schoolgirls waved torches in unison creating fanciful patterns in the gathering darkness and the scoreboard, where I first saw the Olympic Creed, spelled out "SAYONARA."

For that brief moment, as we stood in the darkened infield, young, strong, passionate, we felt within ourselves a strength for human good, greater than that of any individual. We were on a high, but it wasn't grass or booze; it came from within—it was love. We knew that with love and goodwill and youth and energy we

Olympic flame at the Closing with the Japanese moon presiding.

could make a decisive difference in a world too often dominated by the Four Horsemen of the Apocalypse.

We—German, Soviet, Ethiopian, American—were the world's fittest, fastest, strongest, and for that magic moment, we were all-powerful in a harmony that transcended our national origins, and the centuries of traditional hatreds, fears, prejudices, and animosities each of us bore as his heritage.

Did everyone feel that moment as I did? I'm sure not. Would it dissipate? Of course. But I felt it. I know it was real. I savored it, and saved it. For me it was the moment of triumph that might more properly have occurred after our final.

No matter, as the flags were lowered, the Olympic flame slowly extinguished, and the full Japanese moon took over to light our parting, my Olympics were complete.

AFTERWORD

AFTER THE FLAME WENT OUT THAT LONG-AGO NIGHT in Tokyo, rowing has played a continuing role in my life.

On my circuitous route back to the States after the Games, I raced with my Harvard friend Geoff Picard in a regatta on Repulse Bay in Hong Kong, courtesy of the Royal Hong Kong Yacht Club; rowed with significant lack of distinction in Sydney Harbor and on the Yarra River in Melbourne; and coached the Iolani School crews in Honolulu in their annual showdown with Punaho, their private school rivals.

Back home in Michigan and attempting to make a life as a journalist—win a Pulitzer—I got a call from Kell in '66 inviting me to be the press attaché on a State Department trip billed as featuring "the U.S. Gold Medal crew." The junket started on the Nile at Cairo, continued through Eastern Europe (Yugoslavia,

1966, Cairo—Members of the U.S. gold medal eight assess the competition on the Nile.

Bulgaria, Romania), and wound up at the Henley Royal Regatta in England, where Vesper lost to an East German eight. The upshot of that trip for me was that the Big Budd and I decided to train for the 1968 Mexico Games in the coxed pair—an effort ultimately thwarted when I sustained a low-back injury that required surgery.

By 1968, married with two children and practicing law in rural Michigan, my rowing days were finally over. Or so I thought.

To fill the rowing void I tried my hand at guiding and influencing the sport at the institutional level, but soon found myself out of my league among the veterans in the American rowing hierarchy and left them to their deliberations.

Instead I found solace in writing for *The Oarsman*, the American rowing magazine of which the Big Budd was the editor. For a decade or more in the '70s and '80s, no issue (women's rowing was just establishing itself in the face of continuing male chauvinism), or character (Harvard's long time coach Harry Parker, for whom I had great respect, was a favorite subject) escaped my pen.

But two important events served to end my retirement, the first, the installation of a rowing ergometer in my basement, allowing me to get

into racing shape at home, the second, a challenge by a couple of vintage Australian oarsmen to race in the FISA Veterans Regatta in Heidelberg in the fall of 1981.

That challenge signaled the birth of the Compote Rowing Association (a mixture of fruits and nuts in a sauce), a coxed four of like-minded friends and compatriots with whom I raced for

1997, South Australia—Celebrating with my brother Bill after winning in the Compote four in Adelaide.

1995, Slovenija—The Compote pulling away from the winners dock after racing on Lake Bled, the most beautiful racing venue I ever rowed on.

1996, Detroit—After running one leg with the Olympic flame prior to the Atlanta Games. I wore my 1964 racing shirt under the one provided by Coca-Cola.

Christening ceremony at the Vesper Boat Club with my wife Christina, daughter Lucy Dougherty, and son-in-law Michael Dougherty.

most of 25 years in cities around the world from Perth to Prague.

Interspersed throughout those years were four or five tries in the Head of the Charles Regatta, the three mile head race on Boston's Charles River. My first effort resulted in tipping over in a single scull in front of the Cambridge Boat Club with a half mile or so to go; the others were even less noteworthy, depending on your rowing value system.

My Olympic credentials have offered varied opportunities, such as providing color commentary in the early '80s for CBS Sports' coverage of the Oxford/Cambridge Race in London, and carrying the Olympic flame on its long journey from Athens, Greece, to Atlanta, Georgia, for the 1996 Games.

In a sign of advanced age, two racing shells have been named for me, one, a coxed four donated to the Vesper Boat Club by my daughter Lucy Dougherty, the second, another four, donated to Yale by Dr. Ron O'Connor, a coxswain at Yale in the early '60s.

Along the way I attended Kell's funeral in 1985 in Philadelphia's

Fairmount Park (boats from all the boat houses on the Schuylkill rowed over the course in solemn procession, that from Vesper with an empty seat), and delivered the eulogy for Bill Knecht in Camden, New Jersey in 1992. More recently Robby Zimonyi died in 2004, and Tom Amlong passed away in 2009.

Many of my vintage still race competitively, but I am satisfied to give the occasional talk to interested groups, and attend school, college, or boat

club reunions. If the river isn't frozen—as thankfully it was in January, 2014, at Vesper's 50th anniversary celebration of our victory in Tokyo—we usually find enough live bodies to fill a boat and disturb the water gently with our oars.

At one such reunion, my Groton School 55th a few years

2011. The '56 Groton A Boat fifty-five years later on the Nashua River.

back, we were obliged to have the girls' crew put the boat in the water for us, with one of them steering us downstream for half a mile. Upon our return to the dock she reported to her teammates that we were "cute."

"Cute." It's almost enough to make you hang up your oar.